Out on FOOT

Nightly Patrols and Ghostly Tales of a U.S. Border Patrol Agent

Rocky Elmore

published by

duffin|creative

los angeles

Published in the USA by
Duffin Creative
11684 Ventura Blvd #205
Studio City, CA 91604
Visit us on the Web at duffincreative.com

ISBN-10: 0692488383
ISBN-13: 978-0692488386

Printed in the United States of America

Table of Contents

*Images

Out On Foot

"Put loyalty to the highest moral principles and to country above loyalty to persons, party, or Government department."
—*Officer's Handbook M-68, page 4, Code of Ethics for Government Service*

If only Washington bureaucrats and politicians would read the ethics manual and act accordingly!

This book is dedicated to my son Alexander:

May your seas be calm and your winds be fair.

But when life brings a storm, trust in God, and go a little bit Viking!

Introduction

Dear Reader:

At the end of my career, I set out to write a book in order to share with the general public some of my amazing experiences. One of my goals was not to impress my readers, or bore them for that matter, with an "I Love Me" book about endless heroics and law enforcement stories. My intention is not to convince the reader of anything, and I have no particular agenda. I mean simply to share my stories. True, throughout my career I have done my share of those things, as it is quite difficult to serve as a field agent for twenty years on the U.S./Mexico border and not get into a real spot or two. However, for legal reasons I cannot share the majority of those stories. Instead, I wish to give some insight into the world of the Border Patrol agent and demonstrate how vastly different it is from other law enforcement agencies worldwide. Picture it like a very dark version of Alice in Wonderland, if you will, because for ten to twelve hours each day my fellow agents and I stepped into some kind of parallel universe entirely incompatible with the world in which we spent the other twelve.

Many people honestly believe they understand the Border Patrol agent's world, but I can assure you, unless they have been agents, they do not. There is no real understanding of that world without plunging deeply into it on a full-time basis; and I am not talking about going on a three- or four-hour border tour that some politicians brag about, either. Politicians love to fly over the border in a helicopter or take a drive along the fence in a convoy of vehicles for protection and then proudly proclaim, "I've been down in the trenches with those guys, and I know what it's like down there." Truth is, they have been nowhere near the real action, and they know nothing about what it is truly like down there. To those of us who know, their "experiences" are completely laughable.

My main goal with this book is to break ground, so to speak, and open a new door. To my knowledge, few, if any, law enforcement books offer true accounts of on-duty paranormal activity. This is my story blended with a collection of non-fiction tales regarding ghosts, apparitions, or spirits—whatever you wish to call them—as well as a lesser telling of possible Bigfoot and Sasquatch sightings.

All accounts in this book originated with active Border Patrol agents, including my own experiences; therefore, no living agent's real name is used and for good reason. No active duty agent would dare breach this subject publically due to risk of damage to his or her career. Such a faux pas could result in reduced or nonexistent promotion potential as well as the inheritance of titles such as "Loon" or "Nut." Once upon a time, that was important to me, but I am happily retired now and no longer have to concern myself with promotion potential. I also don't mind being called a "Loon" or a "Nut." Trust me, I've been called worse.

If you have faith in God, strong spirituality, or have even a basic grasp of the afterlife, then you understand the concept of dimensions beyond the one in which we live. It should not be hard to believe that other dimensions can, and often do, cross or bump into ours. I know of many law enforcement officers and soldiers who encountered the occasional supernatural situation, but at the Brown Field Station, we experienced far more paranormal activity than any average station. Of that, I am confident. I believe if everyone remains quiet and nobody ever shares their stories, then these tales become lost in time. Such stories are taboo and rarely, if ever, documented. Of that, I am equally confident. However, I have shared some of these tales as they occurred with family and friends, leaving them utterly amazed and often speechless. For years, those close to me have begged me to write this book, but I dared not while still an active duty agent.

Unfortunately, or fortunately depending on your perspective, I do not have enough specifically paranormal stories to fill an entire book; therefore, I added a handful of the more memorable "war stories" to the pile. So here it is! I hope you enjoy reading this as much as I enjoyed experiencing it!

"Honor First"
Senior Patrol Agent, Rocky Elmore, (Ret.)

Chapter 1
Swearing In
The Journey Begins

June 6th has always been a sacred day in American history, especially to me. Of course, I am speaking of the Normandy Invasion on June 6, 1944—D-Day. This moment in history is the subject of many movies, documentaries, and countless horrific stories. Each tale recounts the absolute horror and carnage that the first waves of American soldiers faced on Omaha beach, the worst sector of all. Yet, it is also a story of incredible bravery and courage from a group of men, some barely reaching nineteen years old. These stories are especially significant to our family. You see, my uncle Edgar "Bud" Kimball was a soldier in the 29th Infantry Division, 116 Regiment, Company A.

That's right. He was among the very first wave of American soldiers to land on Omaha beach in northern France. Uncle Bud was killed in combat that day along with the majority of A Company, which was almost completely wiped out. Only a handful of those men survived beyond the first few minutes. My Border Patrol career was, and will forever be, linked to this day—a most bittersweet honor.

On the 50th anniversary of D-Day, June 6, 1994, I entered on duty with the U. S. Border Patrol. The start of such an adventure in my life coinciding with this most monumental day in American history meant everything. Nothing would ever be the same for me again.

I first applied for the position in 1988. In May of 1994, six years later, I received a letter from the United States Border Patrol offering me a position as a Border Patrol Agent (Trainee) at the Brown Field Border Patrol Station in San Diego Sector, San Diego, California. Admittedly, I was reluctant to accept the offer, at first. I had lived in San Diego before and had no desire to return. It was crowded and the cost of living was too high. However, I did have some family there and thought I might try it, at least for a while. So, I set off. It was California or bust.

Joining the Border Patrol did not turn out to be the financial windfall that I hoped it would. I came into the Patrol with nothing and still have most of it. Right away after arriving in California, I discovered many Border Patrol agents actually qualified for food stamps! Indeed, during my first three years in the Patrol I had considerable financial difficulties and often wondered if California was the right place for me. Yet, I kept plugging. I was not in this for the money; I was in it for the adventure, service to the country, and, of course, future retirement benefits.

My fellow new recruits and I had two solid days of filling out forms, orientation, paperwork, information documentation, and then we finished up by filling out some more forms before the final swearing in of our oaths. On the third day, around five o'clock in the morning, we reported to Sector Headquarters in Chula Vista, California. Once there, we hopped on a bus, took off for the San Diego Airport, and boarded a plane bound for Glynco, Georgia. It was one of the longest days of my life.

During the entire day's journey, we were served one sandwich. On the flight to Georgia, I sat next to another recruit named Jim who was from

California. Jim was about six feet and six inches tall and weighed around 260 pounds. I am certain he was the only man on the plane suffering from worse hunger pangs than I was.

Our plane landed in Jacksonville, Florida, where a second bus was waiting to take us to Glynco, Georgia. We could not wait to get to Jacksonville! There would surely be a restaurant at the airport where we could finally sit down and get something to eat. We had it all planned out—a satisfying meal, stimulating conversation.

But that isn't what happened.

The plane landed late in Jacksonville and the bus, apparently tired of waiting for us, was revving up its engine and ready to go. We marched straight through the airport, boarded the idling bus, and took off. There was no time for that leisurely meal in a restaurant. After another hour and a half drive, we finally arrived at our destination—the Federal Law Enforcement Training Center in Glynco. At last, Jim and I could finally get something to eat! We were both really hurting by now and were certain death-by-starvation was near. It was about then that the Border Patrol Academy Instructors informed us that the mess hall had closed just a few minutes before we arrived. "However," they added helpfully, "if it makes you feel any better, we wouldn't have allowed you eat anyway because you haven't processed-in yet. You're not allowed in the mess hall until you have processed in!"

That word "process," and every form of it, quickly became a word I learned to hate!

We processed in and then processed in some more and continued processing in until well after three o'clock in the morning. By then, I was so tired and so hungry I would have killed your favorite cousin for a grilled cheese sandwich! The good news, however, was now we had two whole hours to ourselves and could do whatever we wanted, just as long as we were back up by 5:30 in the morning to get ready for our first day at the United States Border Patrol Academy.

And…that just happened to be when the mess hall opened.

Approximately fourteen seconds after 5:30 a.m., Jim was pounding on my door, yelling, "Get your butt out here and let's go eat!" Certainly, there was no need for Jim to shout. I was already dressed and wondering what was taking him so long. I sprang from the door as if conducting an evacuation drill and we raced to the most important building at the Academy.

The Mess Hall.

Chapter 2
The Academy
Up to Our Necks

During our stay at the Federal Law Enforcement Training Center (FLETC) in Glynco, Georgia, all trainees were required to live on base. While there, we received basic training in things specific to the Border Patrol and law enforcement in general. From the first week of June until the last week of October, we were immersed in firearms training—firing thousands of rounds through .357 Magnum revolvers, 12-gauge pump shotguns, and fully automatic M16 rifles. Then, there was high-speed pursuit driving, coupled with miles and miles of running in the hot Georgia sun. We learned arrest techniques, self-defense, role-playing, as well as immigration and criminal law. The toughest of them all, though, was Spanish. Non-Spanish speaking agents had eighteen weeks to learn this foreign language well enough to use it

5

in life and death situations. It was a most intense experience and a very full five months.

Seniority and Its Perks

Seniority is something that starts immediately upon entering on duty. When newbies arrive at FLETC they are often greeted by the senior class, whose favorite pastime is having a good laugh at newbie expense, engaging in smack talk, and simply messing with the inferiors. Three weeks later, another class will arrive and the new senior class moves into position to mess with the young'uns, because now they have seniority.

Border Patrol academy is a little bit like the military in that they march in formation calling cadence everywhere they go. This formation breaks ranks for nobody. If one group is marching on the sidewalk from the chow hall to the gym, then everyone else had better get off the sidewalk and let them pass. If a formation meets a class senior to its own, then the section leader will lead the class off to the side and give way to the senior class.

One extremely hot and humid afternoon, our class, the 267th, was marching back from the gym towards our classroom when, just up ahead, we saw one of the junior classes marching straight at us. Unbelievably, they were not getting off the sidewalk to let us pass. It was obvious they were unaware of proper sidewalk etiquette and a lesson was in order. As we marched ever closer to the inferior bunch, their section leader led his squad halfway off the walkway. I am sure he was thinking our section leader would do the same and we would share the walkway. Not so! We were senior, and the walkway was ours. A few steps later, we crashed into the other class, much to their surprise and, after some pushing and shoving, order was restored. Both classes continued on their way.

Lesson learned.

Each academy class was divided into two different halves, Section A and Section B. The instructors loved to play both sections against each other. Of course, each section thought it was the best. I was in Section A. Enough said.

Finally, the day both sides had been waiting for arrived. Section A was leaving the gym and Section B was going to the gym. Both were on the same sidewalk. We were all the senior class at the academy, and neither section had real seniority over the other. There was also just enough jealousy between the two sections that neither was willing to give way for the other. As we started to close in on the other half of our classmates, we encouraged our section leader not to share the sidewalk with Section B. They could either move out of our way or fight us over it.

Okay, but there's going to be trouble," the section leader warned. "We're gonna pay for this."

"Yeah, we know," we all assured him. But we didn't care.

Laughing, our section prepared for the inevitable collision.

As expected, Section B felt the same about sharing the sidewalk. When we got close enough to see the other section's faces we discovered they were smiling too, apparently having just had the same conversation.

This was going to be fun!

Sure enough, neither side budged—not even an inch—and Section A crashed head-on into Section B. There was pushing, shoving, random elbows, and even a few kicks thrown into the fray. The game was to stay on the cement. No easy feat! Anyone who managed felt like King of the Mountain, while those who landed in the dirt…not so much. I am not sure if either side officially won that little melee, but I kept both my feet on the cement that day. I felt pretty good about it. It was quite a spectacle anyway, and we loved every moment of it. A good time was had by all. Moreover, to all the other agencies and junior classes watching from the parade grounds, a very clear message was sent: Get off our sidewalk!

Unfortunately, several supervisors and instructors from the Marshals Service, Central Intelligence Agency, and the Customs Service witnessed the event. Never having experienced any fun themselves, these stuffed shirts failed to find the humor in it. Indignant phone calls were made to Border Patrol Instructors regarding concerns over such vile behavior, which was "unprofessional" and quite "embarrassing" to the academy. Requests were made that both sections be appropriately punished. Of course, our class instructors were "appalled" about the incident and promised to take care of it. "This will never happen again," they assured, crossing their fingers behind their backs.

We had not finished marching to our next class when Border Patrol Instructors caught up with us on the parade grounds. We were assigned countless pushups and other painful exercises, while the Instructors yelled and screamed at us, lecturing the whole time on how to behave like true gentlemen and respectable agents. At one point, we were ordered to hold a half-pushup position for several minutes. People's arms eventually reached muscle failure and some collapsed to the ground. My arms were visibly shaking, and I was struggling to hold the horrid position when one of the Instructors singled me out.

He screamed, "Elmore, you scored a one hundred on the law test yesterday, but now you can't even do one pushup!"

That was the last straw. I could not pretend to take this punishment seriously anymore. I burst into hysterical laughter and I, too, collapsed to the ground.

It was contagious.

The phony anger gave way to laughter, consuming Instructors and trainees alike. They weren't mad, they never had been. After all, this was exactly the kind of fight and spirit they wanted to see. These trainees would soon venture out into the mountains and canyons to do this very thing every night for real—conquer obstacles. To survive out there, they needed the level of determination demonstrated here.

The Academy was a little tougher back then and, right before graduation, the PT Instructors paired everybody up and had them fight each other. Boxing, they called it. Section B held their fights in the morning and Section A held theirs in the afternoon. The guys in Section A were typically a little older than the guys in Section B, and many of us were not quite the Greek Adonises we had once been. The PT Instructors took delight in reminding us of that. However, when it came time to put on the gloves, a few guys from Section B were a little reluctant to mix it up—or so said the PT Instructors.

Section A made amends for that. In fact, two or three participants were carted off to the hospital for treatment after their matches. It was a good time. The Instructors enjoyed it immensely and referred to it as a real "Smoker"! They even took back most of the things they had said about our previous sandbagging. Back then, all the fights were videotaped. In the old days, the Instructors would gather at night with a cold beer and enjoy the fights a second time. Of course, they assure us now that is no longer the case.

Yeah right!

Then We Learned The Law

One of the first things we learned in the Academy was important legal definitions, such as the meaning of the word alien. An *alien* is "any person not a citizen or national of the United States."

That includes all persons coming here on immigrant and nonimmigrant visas. If a person is here on a student visa, special work permit, or a visitor's visa, he or she is an alien. Even a person that comes here as a "Lawfully Admitted Permanent Resident" is still an alien, subject to deportation. Notice the older example of an LAPR card below, or green card, says "alien." It does not say "immigrant."

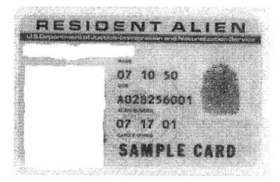

An *immigrant*, by definition, is someone who comes to America and

9

acquires "citizenship" through legal means. If you examine the green card above, you will notice a number in the middle of the card. This number has a letter A at the beginning of it. Until this person acquires citizenship, this will always be the letter A. The A stands for Alien Registration number, not Immigrant number. No matter what kind of visa it is, until a person becomes a U.S. Citizen, he or she will always have an Alien Registration number.

Which brings us to the next point.

There are virtually *no* undocumented persons in the United States, legal or illegal. A few illegal aliens do slip through undetected; however, most are caught, often repeatedly. Once these people are caught, they are processed and documented—documented as being *illegal*, that is.

So, the politically correct statement of an "undocumented immigrant" is utterly preposterous. It is a slap in the face to all the men and women in green who lost their lives performing their duties. They died in defense of America. I knew many of these extraordinary men and women personally. They left behinds wives, husbands, children, brothers, sisters, parents, and their entire futures. Their families deserve better than to hear politicians and news media outlets refer to illegal aliens as simply "undocumented immigrants."

All illegals are aliens, and virtually all are documented; therefore, they will never be referred to as 'undocumented immigrants' in this book. If you are unable to tolerate speech beyond the borders of trendy political correctness, then I encourage you to seek a different book for your entertainment. You will not enjoy this one.

A Powerful Lesson

Another lesson that sticks out in my mind is one of the most important of all: Officer Safety taught by a FLETC instructor. This instructor worked for the Federal Law Enforcement Training Center, not for the Border Patrol, but had previously been a Border Patrol agent. He knew very well what lay ahead for us. Officially, he was there to teach us about drug testing procedures— or maybe it was fingerprinting. I can't remember, because the lesson he so vividly taught us had nothing to do with the subject we had gathered for. This instructor had also been in the U.S. Army Special Forces, or "Green Berets," and served two tours of duty during the Vietnam War.

"I thought I was one tough dude," he told us, deviating from his topic. "I could survive anything. Nothing scared me. When I got out of the army, I joined the Border Patrol. After what I had been through with the military, I certainly wasn't afraid of a few illegal aliens. I had years under my belt and had caught hundreds of aliens without incident. I was tough.

"So one night, just before dusk, I spotted a couple of illegals coming my way. My guard wasn't up at all. In fact, I had arrested these two men a year earlier, and they had offered no resistance at the time. I walked right up to them—the best of friends, not a care in the world—but this time, things turned out differently."

The instructor continued, his tone a sober one. "When I got close, they both jumped me. No warning. During the fight, I heard gunshots and felt a bullet strike my side. I reached for my own gun to return fire, but it wasn't there. They had taken it from my holster and shot me with my own weapon before I even knew it was missing. I managed to get free and did something I had never done before. I left "tough" behind and ran for my life. I was unarmed and badly wounded, and had no way of fighting back. I was very fortunate to have survived that attack and, lest you think I made this up to scare you, here is the newspaper article from that incident."

The instructor then produced a copy of the original newspaper article and left us with a very clear reminder: "Anytime you are dealing with anyone as a law enforcement officer, it is serious business!"

I believe he went on to say that was also his last day on duty as a Border Patrol agent.

As they say: A wise man learns from the mistakes of others. I might have forgotten what the man was there to teach that day, but I never forgot what he said!

A Harsh Lesson, Off the Record

One of the cruelest lessons we learned at the academy, it turns out, was not part of any official curriculum. It was a passive lesson taught by cruel design. This lesson we had no say in, though we utilized it throughout our careers.

We learned to become sociopaths.

Beginning day one of the academy, we built friendships and bonds with our classmates. From sun up to sundown, no matter what we were doing, there was always somebody else wearing green nearby, doing the very same thing. Trainees rarely had a moment to themselves, so we became acquainted fast. In 1994, there were fewer cell phones than today, and no telephones at all in our dorm rooms. With such limited outside contact, it didn't take long to start making friends.

That was bad.

The problem with these friendships was not the manner in which they began but in how they ended. As a class, we embarked in difficult, very stressful situations and were expected to help each other get through them. We learned teamwork. As a result, we began to care about our classmates and viewed them as friends we would retain for life. Sadly, academies are not designed for group success. The program is a weeding process and it is intended for some to fail. When the inevitable would happen, the Border Patrol used this trimming as a terrific opportunity to instill a certain "coldness" into the remaining prospective agents.

So, let's say everyone took a very important test yesterday and we are expecting to get our results back sometime this afternoon. This morning, however, we are being evaluated on water rescue techniques in the pool. After the morning lesson, we meander down to the mess hall and enjoy lunch together, talk a little smack about who doesn't know how to swim, and imagine not a care in the world. After lunch, we return to class for a stimulating lecture on drugs or something. Very routine.

Or so we think.

Then, about ten minutes or so into the class, two Academy Instructors appear in the doorway and ask to see, let's say, Trainee "Whitehead" in the hallway for a moment. Initially, no one thinks anything about it, but, after a couple of minutes, everyone begins to notice that Whitehead has not returned to the classroom. When the last class of the day ends, several of us venture to Whitehead's room to see if everything is okay. We knock on the door, but he does not answer. The shades are open. We look through and find his room empty. We never see or hear from Trainee Whitehead again.

I have to say this lesson stung a little, as Trainee "Whitehead" and I had often become friends.

It usually happened this way. A trainee would fail some part of the course. Two Instructors would arrive during class and ask for Trainee Whomever to step into the hallway. The now ex-Trainee was led directly to the dorm room and told to quickly pack up his or her things. The Instructors would watch while this person packed, forbidding contact with anyone else during the process. Once the ex-trainee was finished, he or she was escorted to a bus, driven to the Jacksonville, Florida, airport, and sent home. No goodbyes, no phone numbers, and no explanations for the sudden departure of these men and women ever occurred. They were just gone.

By the time we arrived at our assigned stations, we understood that nearly all friendships within the Border Patrol were temporary. Agents lived in the moment and in that moment only. People would come and go continually throughout our careers, and it was not wise to become attached.

Here is an example of how fast agents came and went in the San Diego Sector during the 1990s. Around 1995 or 1996, I was told that the Imperial Beach Station had hired 400 new agents for the year. However, they had just lost 404 throughout the same year. Their net loss was four agents.

I have worked with thousands of agents throughout my career. Unfortunately, I can only remember just a handful of these men and women specifically. Many times in this book, I will refer to someone as just an "agent." I mean no disrespect; I simply do not remember all of their names. We were friends and partners within the station and on the field, but once they were gone, we rarely ever saw or heard from each other again. This was the purpose of that harsh passive lesson in the academy. We didn't like it, but we understood it. An active agent simply cannot allow the emotional connection. If a person is to survive this line of work, he or she must learn to adopt at least some of these basic sociopathic behaviors. This is extremely important when handling prisoners and criminal contacts, because, I assure you, suspects use these very behaviors against both their victims and law enforcement officers. In a sense, we are merely two different sides of the same coin. Kind of like yin and yang, I suppose.

Yet, despite all that sociopathic indoctrination, career agents do still manage to make some lifelong friends. When this happens, the bond is strong and they become as close as brothers and sisters.

Chapter 3
Back to the Station
Things Get Tougher

A fter graduating from the academy, we all returned to the Brown Field Station in San Diego. Once there, we started our station and field training programs. We had mistakenly assumed that the hard part was over, when in reality, the hard part was about to begin. Part of the training program was to learn Border Patrol lingo and the 10-codes, as they are called. I cannot share all of them, but I will share a few. These terms are mostly useful for talking on the radio, reading this book, and just sounding cool in general.

Below is a list of some of the things one might hear on the radio, along with a little bit of Border Patrol slang. Hopefully, this will assist you while reading this book.

Useful PA Lingo:

<u>Out on Foot</u>—For officer safety purposes unique to the Border Patrol. This radio call is to let dispatch know an agent will be out of his vehicle, usually hiking around alone deep in a canyon or some other remote area. The dispatcher will then call and do periodic safety checks. If the agent doesn't answer up, a search party is quickly sent to find out why.

<u>War Stories</u>—The retelling of exciting and heroic events, usually in the form of bragging to other agents, family, friends, and women in bars for the purpose of impressing them.

<u>Otay</u>—Pronounced "Oh-tie." This refers to Otay Mountain, Otay Valley, and Otay Lakes. This was our work area.

<u>Star Number</u>—The call-sign used to identify an agent in reference or to speak with another agent over the radio. Names are never used. My first Star Number was Bravo 259, my last was Tango 217, and there were many others in between.

<u>PA</u>—Short for Border Patrol Agent. We usually referred to each other as PAs more so than agents. Other terms less often used to identify agents are BP unit, Green Shirt, or just Green.

<u>NUG</u>—New Ugly Guy, meaning new PA or trainee.

<u>Muster</u>—Daily briefing given to update agents before they head out to the field to start operations.

<u>Go Get A Cup</u>—Going to the nearest convenience store to get a cup of coffee. Very important to say this on the radio as it makes you sound "salty."

<u>Salty</u>—An agent who has been in service for a long time, seen it all, and done it all. His uniform is covered in salt stains and his green shirt is faded to almost white from sun exposure.

<u>La Migra</u>—Border Patrol.

<u>Pollo</u>—Illegal alien. A term used by the smugglers, not so much by PAs.

<u>Pollero</u>—Smuggler. Guide. Coyote. A term used more by the aliens, not PAs.

<u>TBS</u>—Turned Back South. As agents approach, the suspects would often turn around and run south toward the border. Their objective was to avoid arrest by running back into Mexico before getting caught.

<u>Charlie Foxtrot</u>—This one is a bit more common, but if you are unfamiliar with this term, it basically means a really big mess or Cluster F***.

<u>Sientense</u>—Spanish command telling more than one person to sit down. Absolutely the most important Spanish phrase any agent ever learns. Agents must get everyone to sit down on the ground. Nobody is allowed to stand when agents are so vastly outnumbered. Once this command is given, if it is not immediately complied with, then violence is sure to follow on some level. By ignoring this command, the suspects make their intent known, that they will physically resist any arrest attempt. This could result in nothing more than a controlled take down or a possible fight after a foot pursuit, but the potential is there for something much more serious. Either way, it all starts with this one phrase.

Ten Codes:

<u>10-3</u>—Disregard the last order or stop pursuing the action, etc.

<u>10-4</u>—Affirmative.

<u>10-7</u>—Out of service, vehicle or radio is broken, etc. If this is spoken in conjunction with a person or agent's welfare, then the agent or person has either been killed or is already dead.

<u>10-15</u>—Apprehended alien or suspect in custody. 10-15 times 2 would mean two aliens in custody, 10-15 times 60 would be sixty aliens in custody, etc. Soft count of 30 means around thirty suspects. Hard count of 30 means exactly thirty suspects.

<u>Lay-In</u>—One or two agents pick a trail, canyon, or ridgeline, take a concealed position, and wait for traffic to arrive. A PA may stay there all day or all night if necessary.

<u>Traffic</u>—Illegal aliens, drug smugglers, bandits, and/or Rip Crews.

<u>Group</u>—A suspected group of illegal aliens.

Rip Crew—Usually, very experienced hardcore and heavily armed bandits or drug cartel members trying to take down and rob drug loads from opposing cartels. Often, these are cold-blooded killers and are undoubtedly an agent's greatest safety threat.

10-42—Off duty or "End of Watch." On an agent's last workday before retirement, he will often call the dispatcher on the radio at the end of his shift and broadcast that he is 10-42, signifying that his career has ended. 10-42 is also called out at a funeral in conjunction with the individual's Star Number, meaning that the Agent's watch has ended permanently because of his or her death.

Chapter 4
The Field Training Unit
Be Back for You in the Morning!

The first thing we learned on the Field Training Unit was how to lay-in. On Patrol Group A, there were about twenty or twenty-five agents on the training unit at the same time. There were neither enough training officers nor vehicles for all of us, so we piled into a couple of transport vans and rode out to the designated work area for the night. Usually, for every four or five trainees, there would be one training officer in attendance for at least part of the night.

The vans would drive us all out to the mountain, valley, or lake areas, stop near some trail, and a Field Training Officer (FTO) would call out a couple of names. Whoever was chosen would work this canyon or trail for the night. The FTO would have these trainees exit the van and then assure them, "We will be back for you in the morning."

So there we'd be, stranded all night on foot: No sack lunch, no coffee, not even a lawn chair to sit on! Hopefully, a trainee had the foresight to bring a canteen filled with water or maybe a pack of Red Man chewing tobacco to kill some time. We would find a good bush to use for concealment and then just watch and wait and hope it didn't rain! Usually, we didn't have to wait long before a group of illegals came down the trail. The game was hide and seek and, once it started, we were busy all night. I cannot remember anything that was ever as much fun as the games we played on those nights.

If, by chance, a trainee was not ejected somewhere along the way but instead remained in the van, he or she would stay with a Field Training Officer and typically end up hiking up the mountains or down in the valleys all night. FTOs were not too fond of just hiding behind a bush for ten hours like some kind of night stalker waiting to ambush someone on the trail. Patience, however, is a plus, and picking a good hiding spot never hurt either. It was easier to catch more people by waiting than by hiking around all night searching for them, but that could be boring. "A broke clock is right twice a day, but if it's five minutes off, it's wrong all day long." It may be a cliché, but it certainly is true in this line of work. For instance, an agent walking the right trail at the wrong time would miss all the action, whereas the agent lying in wait got to play.

Hiding in the bushes all night long waiting to jump the next passerby could eventually make an agent feel rather ghoulish. The fact is, after a while, a person starts to become the bogeyman he once feared and, worse, start to like it a lot! I cannot imagine any other job where the sole purpose is to conceal oneself in the deepest woods during the dead of night, lying in wait to jump out and make physical contact with total strangers without warning. I must say that even as high risk as this activity can be, it becomes quite addictive.

Often, it wasn't even necessary to hide or "bush-up." If it was dark enough, we could simply stand out in the open and, in some places, the illegals would just walk right up to us, assuming were some dumbbell who had gotten lost from the group and just standing there trying to figure out what to do next. On really dark nights, they usually could not see our badges, patches, or gun belts. If the group was small enough, we could bust them when they walked up and take them into custody right then. If the group was too big, which it often was, we might join in the back of the line and start walking along with them without their knowledge. This was just too funny! Sometimes, it was all I could do to keep from laughing aloud as I hiked through the canyons with an unsuspecting group of aliens.

I would simply join in the back of the group and act like one of them. Occasionally, the last person in line would turn around and look back at me in confusion, trying to figure out what was going on. I would put my forefinger over my mouth and whisper, "Shhh!" Then, I would put my hand on his shoulder or hold the back of his collar, and he would stay quiet and not warn the others. If an agent had a soft, low voice like I did, he could easily talk on the radio the whole time, calling out every movement, location, and change of direction. When enough of the other agents got into place, we would take them all down.

Often, the illegals never figured it out!

Counting Numbers

During the first few years of my career, Brown Field was a very busy place. It was not uncommon for the patrol group to arrest 500 to 800 illegal aliens per eight-hour shift during hours of darkness. One night in particular, I was at the station working in the processing area of the jail. It was a swing shift, and our count that evening was 815 apprehensions for Patrol Group A, between 3:00 p.m. and 11:00 p.m. That was the busiest night I personally know of, but that's only because I was working in the processing center that evening and had access to the numbers. I am certain there were other nights even busier than that, I just don't know the numbers for those shifts.

It was common for two or three agents working together to catch as many as 100 aliens between them throughout the course of a shift. This happened on a regular basis. On one occasion, I saw four agents up on the mountain trying to work a group of 300 by themselves. They managed to catch about

21

seventy illegals on the initial takedown. Several more of us went into the area as quickly as we could and, within a few hours, had caught nearly 200 more of them. We only lost about twenty to thirty overall.

Not bad for a day's work.

How to Take a Group Down

The vegetation that covered a large part of our area of operations consisted of Manzanita. If you are unfamiliar with the Manzanita bush, trust me, it is some of the hardest, toughest, and most dense vegetation in the region. This stuff actually punctured a layer or two of my bulletproof vest once. It is extremely thick. The trails running through the Manzanita bushes are often very narrow and, once a person is on a trail lined with this bush, it is not easy to get back off again. We used that to our advantage. By far, the best way to take down a group of illegals was to do an "Ol' Number Six" on them.

An Ol' Number Six would go something like this:

A sensor would bang off. An agent and a partner would go to the trail corresponding to that bug, find a place in the brush to hide, and vanish from sight. The busting agent would be positioned about 100 feet to the north, while other follow up agent would be concealed to the south. The PA to the south would let the group of aliens pass by and then close the gate on them from behind, so to speak. When the group got near, the southern agent would click his mic several times to warn the northern agent of their arrival. If something was amiss, such as the presence of weapons, the southern agent would give him an appropriate early warning. Then, once the group passed, the southern PA would fall in behind them.

This was a basic North/South Lay-in operation.

The northern, or busting, agent would patiently wait for the signal. At night, we always heard the illegals before we saw them and, many times, we never did see them. We just knew how close they were by listening to their footsteps.

When I first began to hear them, my heart would always beat a little bit faster. The closer their footsteps sounded the faster my heart would beat. Anticipation would continue to build, but it was important to remain motionless. My breathing would grow shallow, but I kept absolutely quiet to avoid spooking them, which was hard because it always seemed like the closer they got, the slower they got. Sometimes, I thought the beating of my heart was so loud, the group might hear it and run away before I could jump them. Finally, the guide would be so close, I could simply say in a voice barely more than a whisper, "Sientense todas. La Migra." (Everybody sit down. Border Patrol.)

At that point, the startled guide would freeze for about one second. It is within that single moment, a one-second window, that an agent is able to take the group down. It is a transfer of power—from him to the agent. Of course, it is always best to help the smuggler get down onto the ground as quickly as possible, typically before he can change his mind about being captured. You see, it is all about helping them get their minds right!

As soon as the southern agent senses that his partner has popped the guide, he will physically push the group into a cluster from behind. One PA pushes from the front, the other pushes from the back, sandwiching the illegals in between. Usually at this point, they will just sit down—no yelling or screaming, no flashlights, no drama. If this typical scenario plays out silently and without lights, then others will not realize Border Patrol agents are in the area. This is the goal because, if there are other groups coming up behind them, agents have a chance at those as well. That, my friend, is a textbook take down. You get the guide, you get the group.

It's that simple.

However, if you fail to take the guide in that first second, then he will unlock from his moment of temporary paralysis and run like crazy, taking his group with him. The downside to this type of tactic is that, if the group is armed or decides to go on the offensive, then there is absolutely nowhere for the agent to run and nothing to take cover behind. The agent must shoot it out or fight it out right where he or she stands.

There have been countless Border Patrol shootouts throughout history where PAs have come face to face with armed bandits at point blank range on such trails. Agent and bandit both empty their weapons at an average distance of three to four feet, each taking multiple hits in the process. Sometimes these encounters take place on trails so narrow that the agents and bandits are in single file formation, meaning that even if there are more PAs behind the lead agent and more bandits behind the lead bandit, neither side can fire any weapons without risk of shooting his own buddy in the back. The agent and bandit in the point position of their respective lines may well be the only ones firing shots at each other, while their companions merely watch, until a clear firing opportunity opens up. So, suffice it to say, agents are not the only bogeymen that roam this no-man's-land along the border.

Another tactic we often used up on the mountain was the "Water Jug Tactic." Of course, this works best at night. In the past, virtually every alien hiked up the mountain carrying a one-gallon white or clear water jug (now they carry black ones). Empty jugs were tossed aside by the thousands, leaving litter all over the mountain. My partner and I would grab a couple of jugs off the ground and start hiking up a trail, single file, making sure to bang the jugs around on the bushes a little to make some noise.

There were always groups of aliens laid-up and hiding deep in the bushes that we just couldn't find without a little help. When groups lay-up and hide, they are very quiet and prefer that other groups passing by be quiet as well. Hiking up a trail and making a lot of noise was an excellent way to tick off any groups that were laid-up nearby, especially the guide. As you passed by, they would call out and curse at you, making threats like, "Hey @#$ $%, be quiet or we'll kick your %@#."

Well, it was certainly sweet of them to yell out like that and let us know where they were because, at that point, we would simply walk right over and put an end to their little siesta.

One night, a couple of PAs were engaged in this very tactic, when they noticed a group of aliens with flashlights turned on walking up an adjacent trial nearby. Now this was very unusual, as illegals never used or even carried flashlights. In my entire career, I never once saw a group use lights. Nevertheless, these particular agents recognized an opportunity. They simply turned on their own flashlights, walked up, and joined the back of the unsuspecting group.

They hiked with the illegals for a bit without a single person catching on. A short while later, the foot guide ordered the group to stop and turn off their lights. Everyone obeyed, but then one of the aliens in the group accidentally turned his light back on. It was only for a second, but the enraged guide told the offending man to turn off that %$#@ light or he would come back there and beat him.

Sensing another excellent opportunity, Adrian, one of the two agents, turned his light back on, knowing the enraged guide would come back to punish him. It was the perfect way to take the guide without alerting the group to their presence.

Sure enough, the furious guide screamed at Adrian, cursing and spitting, "I'm coming back there to teach you a lesson, you stupid pollo!"

As promised, the foul-mouth guide stomped his way toward the back of the group.

Adrian turned his light off.

It was clear the fuming smuggler was more than prepared to assault the culprit as he marched angrily closer. However, just as the guide reached striking distance, Adrian flicked his flashlight on and shined it directly into the hostile man's eyes. The smuggler tried to throw a punch. Adrian easily ducked the blow and hit him square in the face. The guide went down and the rest of the group was easy pickins.

You gotta love it when a plan works out!

Years later, while working the Kingsville, Texas Station, a newer agent and I were walking down a road late one night. I noticed that he kept walking beside me, so I informed him that we needed to walk single file. This particular agent was a Star Wars movie buff, and thought I must be one too, as he jokingly commented, "Jedi warriors walk single file. Are we walking single file to hide our numbers, like the Jedi?"

"No, it's to hide our identity," I replied. "Jedi mind tricks would be nice, but we don't have that luxury. To successfully catch aliens, we must learn to think and act like aliens, as well as look and sound like them as we approach."

How Not to Take a Group Down

Time and time again, I witnessed some of the younger Green Shirts trying to take alien groups down by screaming at them from fifty or sixty feet away. There are two typical reasons why a PA would do this: Either the agent was inexperienced and overcome by excitement or was scared and didn't want to get close enough to actually catch the illegals, thereby, yelling and giving the group a chance to escape. Immediately afterward, these same agents would shout into the radio, "I just busted a group up here need some help! They're running all over the place!"

Well, of course they were! Not surprisingly, this always tended to happen to the same handful of PAs. These individuals also seemed never to figure out that everyone, including the aliens, knew they were just scared of getting close. Unfortunately, some of these agents became training officers later on and taught the latest round of trainees to do the very same thing.

There are exceptions, however.

When I worked in the Tucson Sector towards the end of my career, drugs were still being backpacked across the border on foot. Drug smugglers often ran with an armed escort, usually carrying AK-47s. Rip Crews operated on those same trails. Their job was to intercept and rob those same drug smugglers. Their weapon of choice was either an AK-47 or an AR-15. If an agent thought there was any chance the encounter involved working dope with an armed escort or a Rip Crew, it was better to engage from a distance. If I was carrying a rifle and working during daylight hours, I considered seventy yards to be just about right.

If a BP unit was alone and facing long arms with only a pistol, it was best not to engage at all. The procedure was to take a good position and wait for backup. At night, however, the agent doesn't always have that luxury. He may not know what he is facing until it is too late. At this point, the PA is relying entirely on luck as this is far more dangerous, since it puts him or her much too close for a confrontation with long arms. With a little luck a Scope, a night vision camera with a zoom lens, is in the area, because it is times like this when the scope operator can save an agent's life. But, given the chance, smugglers will almost always throw down their drugs, and sometimes their weapons, and try to run away. Then, the agent can start tracking them down in a safer manner. Occasionally, the drug runners would just surrender, but there was no way to know what they would do in advance. It was always best to have a little distance, if possible.

These drug smugglers and Rip Crews operate in groups averaging between five and seven, while an agent might be alone or, at most, have one other PA with him. Sneaking up quietly on armed drug smugglers and Rip Crews, therefore, was not a particularly good idea, as it offered no advantage to the agent. As a result, the best tactic is to give a verbal warning because one cannot simply open fire, except in extremely rare circumstances.

Another reason to give a verbal warning is that it might actually be another agent moving in from a different angle. BP units encounter each other on trails all the time. Without some kind of verbal challenge first, this could easily result in a friendly fire situation. Albeit extremely rare, it does happen.

On the other hand, if the bad guys hear someone sneaking up on them with no verbal challenge, they may assume it is a Rip Crew and panic. If so, they will open fire without warning. An agent at such close range is already heavily outnumbered. In this scenario, the PA is potentially out-gunned as well, so it is far safer to confront this particular group from a distance. If the bad guys decide to shoot it out anyway, the agent seventy yards away has a much better chance of survival than the one at five yards. Hopefully, he or she has already taken a position of advantage, if there is any to be had. The illegals would likely be moving, placing them at a disadvantage. The agent should remain still and quiet regardless because whoever gets heard first, gets ambushed.

Force on force training taught me one thing really well: Shootouts with rifles at very close range and on open ground usually leaves everyone involved with fatal hits, especially when any type of medical assistance could be hours away. Actual shootings that have taken place reinforce this line of thinking. Unless a PA can get an instant first round kill on all adversaries, which is highly unlikely, then the adversaries will have a chance to get a hit on the agent at very close range, often with a high powered automatic rifle. During the stress of a shooting, it is easy enough to miss at five yards with a handgun, but not with a rifle carrying a thirty round magazine. With any luck, one of the cameras or scopes will see the group before a BP unit responds. Then the scope operator can tell the responding agent if it is a drug run or just regular alien traffic, allowing the agent to adjust engagement tactics accordingly. A scope can be your very best friend.

Think back to the carnage caused by the two Los Angeles bank robbers, Larry Phillips and Emil Matasareanu. They held the entire L.A. Police force at bay for hours and paralyzed the whole city, all because they had rifles (CNN, 1997). Border Patrol agents sometimes run into similar scenarios, only they're alone and in very remote areas.

Although I was shot at in sniper-style attacks on two separate occasions while serving at Brown Field, firearms were seldom a problem in the San Diego Sector. We suffered plenty of sniper-style attacks from the south side of the US/Mexico border, but the bandits didn't usually bring their weapons to the north side. The Border Patrol and San Diego Police Department Bandit Teams had taken care of that problem back in the 1980s, when they compiled a body count of Mexican bandits numbering up into the triple digits.

Even though numerous Border Patrol agents were wounded on these anti-bandit operations, no agent had ever been killed. The original Bandit Team had actually been a San Diego Police Department brainchild, but later expanded to Border Patrol and the San Diego Sheriff's Department as well. As far as I know, not a single participating officer from the other departments was ever killed either. This is quite remarkable considering the hundreds of shootings that occurred over the years of operation.

So, Mexican bandits rarely crossed north into the Brown Field Station's area of operations carrying firearms—the price to be paid was simply too high. In thirteen years at Brown Field, I never took a firearm off an illegal alien. However, there was a pattern out there that was just as concerning as any shootout, if not more so.

If the aliens or smugglers decided they wanted to harm or kill a PA, they did not bring a firearm with them. Instead, they tried to take it from the agent and use his own weapon against him. During one period spanning a little more than a year, one or more suspects attacked five different agents. All five incidents resulted in a struggle of some type over the PA's gun with one or more shots being fired. Miraculously, no agents were killed or seriously injured during these incidents. Later, however, there was a sixth incident where the agent was beaten, and the suspect was fatally shot.

Afterward, sometime after I was transferred out of San Diego Sector, Agent Robert Rosas was lured into an ambush while working alone one night. Tragically, he was jumped by multiple suspects, disarmed, and apparently killed with his own weapon.

This was one of the nastier alien tactics, and the one most of us feared more than facing an already armed gunman. I don't know about you, but I would rather shoot it out with my gun than fight over the possession of my gun! This was one area where my brothers and sisters in green seldom let their guard down.

Another tactic often used by the more dangerous criminals was to attack Border Patrol agents with large rocks. Several PAs were ambushed and hit in the head and face with rocks weighing as much as twenty pounds. I knew of three agents who received fractured skulls and/or crushed eye sockets in this manner. An attack by an illegal alien with a rock is a deadly force issue from the very beginning, and, unfortunately, was rather commonplace in the San Diego Sector.

An Unexpected Helping Hand

Usually when a PA goes 10-15 with a group, he or she has to sit and wait with them for a while until transport or other BP units arrive. Often times, while the agents are babysitting the illegals they have already caught, another group will move through directly behind them. Guides do this on purpose. They use the group ahead of themselves somewhat like minesweepers. If they see a flashlight or hear an agent take the bunch down, they will not use that trial again for the rest of the night, but will instead shift the traffic to other trails. If a PA takes a group down quietly and without using his light, then the others will just keep on coming.

However, if a PA is working solo and sitting on a group, how can he or she work another one? Actually, it is very simple. Get the aliens already caught to assist. Now, they won't always help, but you would be surprised how often they will. When I joined the patrol in 1994, most illegal aliens were fairly decent people, not like the influx of criminals and gang members that showed up in great numbers in later years. If the group was respectful and posed no threat, it was common for us to talk and even laugh with them while waiting for transport. If the Guide or Coyote was treating the group badly, which was common, the illegals were often glad to get busted by the Border Patrol, just to end the abuse.

One night, while I was still on the training unit, we were working Otay Mesa. The mesa was merely the flats at the bottom of Otay Mountain, about three miles wide and another three miles long. The FTOs drove us all out in a van and dropped us off one at a time about one quarter or half mile apart. This area was completely flat and covered with grass about two feet high, no trees or bushes to hide behind. Each trainee was left out on foot all night with nowhere to go. So, we just sat down in the tall grass and waited for the traffic and hoped it didn't rain. If we caught a group, the transport van would drive in (lights out), load the illegals up, and then drive 'em away.

After about an hour, I caught my first group. It was about seven or eight people, best I can remember. This group was friendly enough and caused no problems, so the 10-15s and I sat down in the grass and talked while we waited for transport. Soon, I noticed another group coming up, about fifteen or so. I asked the 10-15s if they wanted to help me catch the bunch that was heading toward us.

"Sure," they agreed. "Since we got caught, they should get caught too!"

"Ok, everybody down," I said. "When they get close, call them over."

They all cooperated and laid down like I asked them to, and we waited. One guy got a little restless, but one of the other participants in the group told him to be quiet or he would scare the incoming group off. When the second bunch came within range, one of the 10-15s called out to them. "Compas, vengan para aca (Companions, come over here)," he said.

The unsuspecting group came over, and I gave them the bad news, "Sientanse, La Migra."

Transport was on the way. The first group of 10-15s, who had just helped me, thought it was quite funny and were all laughing about it. Even better, the group they had just helped sucker seemed to find the humor in it as well.

I thought it was funny too.

Working the processing center was about the worst assignment a PA could get, but sometimes the aliens would help out there as well. On an average night during the 1990s, four agents would be assigned to run the processing center. During their shift, they would search and process four or five hundred incoming prisoners. The overwhelming majority of these would be processed and sent right back to Mexico, only to cross again later that night. Once, I caught the same group of twenty-six illegal aliens twice inside of an hour and a half—in the very same place!

Nonetheless, keeping four or five hundred people under control, with only four agents, even for just a few hours, can be quite a challenge, because agents in the jail area are unarmed.

One tactic we would occasionally employ was to pick out two or three of the biggest aliens and "deputize" them. Of course, they weren't really deputized, but it was always funny to watch how serious they usually took it. They would make sure the others prisoners behaved themselves, keep the peace, and even pick up their trash. It wasn't something we did very often, but it was usually good for a laugh when we did. The aliens got a kick out of it too. It was also very helpful.

A Coker Moment

The most unorthodox way I ever heard of a group getting caught happened to a friend of mine on Patrol Group A. One night, when Jay Coker was a trainee, the training unit was working the area around the Otay Mesa Port of Entry. It was a midnight shift and numerous trainees were dropped off on foot around the commercial buildings near the Port of Entry. The training van drove down the street, lights out, and dropped a trainee off on every corner, assigning each his or her own block to work.

Agent Trainee Coker thought he had found the perfect spot to lay-in-wait behind a large utility box with a commercial building about six or seven feet behind him. The box was large enough that he could comfortably stand behind it and wait for customers to come straight to him. But, to his disappointment, all was quiet that night. Although he diligently watched over the top of the utility box all night long, not a single alien came down his street.

Finally, the sun rose. Coker got up and stretched and started moving around a bit. In the process, he looked behind himself and screamed. His shout was heard for several blocks.

Naturally, the other agents came running.

Coker, in the light of day, had turned around to find about fifteen illegal aliens sitting silently behind him against the exterior wall of the building. He had been so excited to find the utility box for cover that he failed to check the bushes behind him with a flashlight to make sure his hiding place was empty. So, not wanting to give away his position, he kept his light off and merely scanned the area with his naked eyes. He'd had no clue the illegals were there.

The aliens didn't speak or try to run off because they assumed the agent knew they were there and believed they had been caught. Patiently and silently, they sat right behind the unsuspecting agent all night.

All that morning, Coker could be heard screaming to the other agents, "They could have killed me!"

As funny as this incident was, however, he was right. If the group had a mind to, they could have easily killed him.

Although Coker was actually a very effective agent, he often had moments like these—Kodak Moments—where you wish you had your camera to record it. So, before long, every time one of these bizarre moments happened, it became known as a "Coker Moment."

And let me tell you, Coker was a real hoot to work with! I was fortunate enough to experience firsthand some of these moments with him myself, and I will remember them for the rest of my life.

Chapter 5
On My Own
Playin' Possum

A s you may have figured out by now, sometimes things don't always go as planned. I don't care how much time and effort someone puts into it, things often fall apart at first contact, especially if there are only one or two agents trying to work a large gathering of illegal aliens, like forty or more. Even smaller groups of twenty or thirty can turn into pure pandemonium. Believe me; Border Patrol agents experience these kind of moments on a pretty regular basis.

Most of the time, pandemonium can be fun. If everything is in total chaos, then there is really no way to mess something up. Right? Well, sometimes PAs have a tendency to take things too seriously, causing themselves a lot of undue stress. I have always told my fellow brothers and sisters in green that nothing is serious, except your safety.

Sal and I were working in Windmill Canyon one night when a plan of ours fell apart. It was a very bright moonlit night, a full moon if I remember correctly, and visibility was excellent. A sensor had hit, and we were laid-in waiting for our customers to arrive. Sal was bushed-up on the side of a hill to my south, while I was hiding couple hundred yards to the north. I had picked a narrow spot in the trail surrounded by heavy brush where I could easily hide until the group arrived. I could then merely step out onto the trail and shut the voyage off. Sal would drop down off the hill with precision timing and move in behind them, leaving the illegals with nowhere to go. It was the perfect plan. No way it could it go awry.

And everything went according to plan…for a while.

Sal spotted the group walking through the brush about three hundred yards south of me. All seemed normal until, suddenly, the group stopped. There was a section of the trail about two hundred yards or so between the group and where I was hiding that was completely exposed. It was great for us, because it was easy to watch, but as the group neared the opening, they also realized how easy it was for anyone to spot them. They were afraid to cross it for fear of being seen, so they just sat down for a while to think about it.

Well, Sal and I didn't have all night. We tried to wait them out, but shift change was coming up and the group knew it. They also knew any agent in the area would have to pull out soon, and they intended to wait us out.

Sal kept giving me updates. "They're still just sitting there," he would say.

Finally, Sal and I both decided to go down and dig them out of the bushes where they were hiding, which meant I would have to cross the 200 yards of open ground with a full moon bearing down on me. A slight bend in the trail partially blocked their vision of the open space, and I figured I might be able to use it to my advantage. So, I left my perfect hiding spot and started walking out in the open, hoping for the best. Sure enough, just as I got to the point of no return, the group decided to get back up and start moving again.

"Bravo 259, they're up and moving again and almost to the bend. Quick, find somewhere to go!" Sal warned.

I stopped and looked around, but there was nowhere to go. Nothing to take cover behind, and it was too far to go back to my original hide. "Crap! Now what am I going to do?" I thought.

Sal's voice crackled over the radio again. "They're starting around the bend now."

I had no more options. I needed to do something right then, and there was no time left. There was a small embankment right where I was standing, so I lay down on the trail with my back against the embankment. I took out my revolver and kept it by my side in case things went bad and decided to play dead, right there on the trail in plain sight. From Sal's position, he could see what I was attempting, so he kept giving me updates over the radio.

"The group is spreading out," he said. "We need to get them back together somehow before you bust them."

About that time, the foot guide walked up to my position. The hard part about playing dead, is keeping your eyes open without blinking. As the guide approached, he looked at me with a rather puzzled look on his face. I stared him right in the eye. The poor guy didn't know what to do, so he just stood there.

Then two or three more walked up, and they all just stood there staring at me, and I at them. They then started discussing whether or not I was really dead before, finally, deciding that I was. All the while, I needed to blink so bad I couldn't stand it anymore. It was becoming unbearable. After what seemed like an hour and a half, but was only maybe a minute and a half, Sal gave me another update.

"Ok, the last one just caught back up with them," he said. "They're all together now."

Finally, I could blink!

Slowly, I sat straight up and, pointing my finger at the guide, said, "Sientense todos!"

The aliens were terrified! They all froze for a second and then sat down on the trail. All but one, anyway, who continued to just stand there, covering his mouth with both hands and gasping for air. He couldn't move. He just stood

37

there shaking, his eyes wide open and his pupils fully dilated. By that time, I had stood up and repeated my order to the quivering alien to sit down with the rest of the group.

All of a sudden, the man dropped his hands from his mouth and pointed his finger at me. "Oh!" he exclaimed in English. "It's you!"

I laughed. "Yeah it's me," I replied, "now, sit down."

At that point, the alien fell to the ground clutching his chest and breathing heavy sighs of relief, while the rest of the group, including myself, broke into hysterical laughter.

I suppose it just took that fellow an extra second or two to realize that I had not truly risen from the dead, but had merely pulled a fast one on him.

Sign Cutting and Tracking

What would a book about the Border Patrol be without sign cutting and tracking? Despite all the advances in technology, it usually still comes down to following footprints. We refer to it as "Sign." I have heard some tracking schools refer to sign as "spoor," but, within the Patrol, it is always known as "Sign."

I have also heard that some civilian tracking schools claim that the Border Patrol is one of their clients. I assure you, no outside source teaches the Border Patrol how to track. PAs learn to track from their training officers and agents that are senior to them. This is not to say that tracking schools do not have some sign cutters that are better than many agents. Depending on which station a trainee serves at, he or she may not learn sign cutting or tracking at all. However, almost all modern day tracking, inside the U.S. at least, originated within the Border Patrol at some point. We have even sent personnel to foreign countries to help their version of border patrol learn sign cutting.

At night, the scope could walk a PA right to where illegals were hiding. If a scope was available and could operate in the area an agent was working, it was by far the best way to go. Yet, in many areas and on most of the mountain, they were unable to operate effectively. In those areas, it was all agent and hopefully some luck. The sensors could get us into the general area, unless it was a false hit, but we still had to find their sign and start tracking.

Tracking is a skill that most agents take great pride in and is the one skill that sets Border Patrol agents apart from all other law enforcement agencies worldwide. There is no more satisfying way to catch bad guys than to track them down to the very bush or abandoned building they're hiding in. They usually don't even know trackers are on their trail until it's too late.

Tracking is not without risk, though. One rule of thumb is: Never track alone. A friend of mine once got so engrossed in following a suspect's tracks that he followed the sign right to a pair of shoes under a tree. Problem being, the suspect was still wearing the shoes and was now standing over him. Whether it happened exactly that way or not, I cannot know. My friend could perhaps have embellished his account a little, but the message was clear.

While discussing the subject in the academy, however, we were told of an agent who was tracking a Mexican bandit somewhere in Arizona. The agent followed the tracks around a bend in the trail and, while looking intensely down at the sign, was shot by the very man he was tracking.

The suspect had noticed the PA following behind at some distance, but the agent was so focused on the sign that he did not realize he had closed in on the suspect. The smuggler simply picked some high ground at a bend in the trail, lay in wait, and took his shot. Fortunately, the agent did survive.

Once, while I was temporarily detailed to the El Cajon Station, the California Highway Patrol (CHP) became involved in a high-speed pursuit with a van full of illegal aliens. It had started well out of town, somewhere near Alpine, I think, and had come to an end near Interstate 805 and Interstate 8. About ten or fifteen illegals bailed out of the van and took off running for the San Diego River bottom. By this time, the CHP had already called for other departments to assist.

Lastly, a radio call went out for Border Patrol assistance. I answered up and informed the radio dispatcher that I was only a few miles out and could head that way.

Actually, I had been quietly following the pursuit about three miles back, the whole time knowing they would crash or bailout before long, and I wanted to be within striking distance when they did. When I arrived at the scene, there must have been at least twenty officers already there. California Highway Patrol, San Diego Police Department, San Diego Sheriff's Department, and a helicopter were all searching the area, but they were not having any luck.

I figured the group would run straight for the water, so I headed for a cane thicket and started looking for their sign on trails running perpendicular to the river. Down in the thicket, I ran into two officers from the San Diego Police Department Tactical Team. These officers were searching the brush, but had not thought to look for footprints. I talked to them for a moment and asked if they had any tracking experience.

"No, we don't," one said.

"If you want to follow me," I offered, "I think we can find them."

The ground was damp and soft along the river bottom, and I figured it would be pretty easy to pick up their trail. The San Diego police officers took me at my word and gladly followed along. In less than three minutes, I had detected soft dirt with fresh sign on it. I told the officers a little about how we typically tracked illegals down, and they seemed to be pretty excited about trying it out. So the three of us started our tracking operation and followed wherever the sign led us.

At times we found ourselves crawling on our bellies underneath bushes and through the mud, but the officers were game for it and even seemed to be enjoying it. When we finally made it to the river, we found the illegals. They were right out in the middle, submerged up to their necks and thinking they had successfully given everyone the slip.

Once the group saw us, they knew the gig was up.

We called the disappointed aliens over and, one by one, pulled them out of the water. The whole operation had taken less than ten minutes. When the three of us walked out of the river bottom escorting the entire group, we were covered from head to toe in weeds and mud. The officers from the other departments were amazed that we had found them so quickly.

However, there were other times where we stayed on alien sign for the entire duration of a shift, eight to ten hours, sometimes following tracks for miles. More often than not we eventually caught up with them, but sometimes they gave us the slip. These may well be some of your neighbors right now! Well, I suppose if we had been successful every time our job wouldn't have been much fun, now would it?

What else is fun? Finding a group sound asleep underneath a tree. After tracking them for hours, this was a reward all in its own. Do you have any idea how much fun it is to grab an unsuspecting, slumbering international traveler by the leg and shake him until he wakes up, while screaming, "Bienvenidos a los Estados Unidos!" (Welcome to the United States).

The look of shock on their faces is priceless! I know, it is a bit mean, but once they calm down, they usually think it's kind of funny too.

I will say, many illegals do have a pretty good sense of humor. Agents and aliens do not always have this adversarial relationship filled with hate like so many people think. It is a serious job, and we take it as such, but at the end of the day, we are all still human beings, capable of sharing a laugh. If an alien's life is in peril, it is the Border Patrol agent that will save him or her, even at the risk of the agent's own life, and these people know it. Often times, for female aliens, a Border Patrol agent is the most welcome sight they have ever seen.

One night, after having a somewhat minor fight with one of the smugglers and getting the best of him, I noticed three or four of the younger women in the group covering their mouths while they watched and realized they were laughing. I took a wee bit of offense to it and demanded to know what they thought was so funny. They grew suddenly very quiet and would not speak.

Then, one of the men in the group asked if he could tell me something privately. I allowed him to and he quietly told me, "The girls are laughing because the guide was very mean to them during our passage. They were very afraid he was going to rape them, so they enjoyed seeing him suffer at your hands."

41

So, I faced the girls and gave them a smile and a nod of approval, and their giggling commenced. This time I did not interrupt them. They deserved to laugh. Like many agents, I have plenty of violent war stories I could tell, but those don't tell the whole story. More importantly, I have rescued plenty and laughed with more illegal aliens than I have ever seriously fought with.

Other than having broken our immigration laws, some of the aliens were quite decent people. This compliment does not include the guides, coyotes, and smugglers. They were all cutthroats.

The Way We Play

As a general rule, Border Patrol agents break every tried and true officer safety rule that all other law enforcement agencies and police departments live by. The amazing thing is, we get by with it. Our world is vastly different from the one in which a local police officer operates. In fact, former police officers often have a hard time adjusting to this line of work and the tactics necessary to work the border. If we followed the same officer safety rules that they do, we simply could not do our jobs. We probably couldn't catch anyone.

Agents learn very early on that Border Patrol is not normal law enforcement and that we must get comfortable with getting very close to suspects, especially in the dark. Walking right up to a suspect without hesitation or fear will usually unnerve the suspect. It gets inside their decision-making process and makes them wonder what the agent is going to do as opposed to focusing on what the suspect had been planning. It distracts them. Criminals are not used to this from law enforcement, as police officers are typically far more reserved and keep a much greater distance. Border Patrol does not always operate that way. We often used aggressiveness as a form of officer safety as it cuts down on time of exposure.

This is not to say that we showed aggression recklessly or carelessly. We just knew always to expect suspects to turn on us and were ready for it when they did. We had to know precisely how we ourselves would react in any situation.

At first, I was a little worried about my easygoing personality. I am not as hot-tempered as other people in this field tend to be, and I thought this might be a problem during some of the more violent physical confrontations. However, I quickly learned that a hot temper serves no purpose in law enforcement, except to get someone into trouble or cause mistakes, often by simply being baited.

When criminals attack officers, they often do it with such blinding speed that there is no time to get mad, regardless of how hot tempered the agent is. Other times they test a few times to gauge a reaction before launching an assault, but, when it comes, it does so with the same ferocity as those that come with no warning.

After multiple contacts and confrontations, most agents learn to just "snap," and take action. We also learn to turn this behavior on and off at will, without the involvement of emotion. This is where the passive sociopathic training we received during the academy comes into play. Criminals do it all the time and good agents are capable of the very same thing. It helps us to react quicker, more decisively, and take the right course of action without emotional interference.

As a training officer, one of the things I stressed most to any new trainee was, "The most dangerous thing any police officer or agent ever does is go into a convenience store for a cup of coffee." This is when his or her guard should be up at its peak, but often the opposite is true and it is completely down. Think about it. How many officers have been killed while taking a coffee or lunch break?

A funny but serious quote we often repeated was, "Be polite, be professional, but have a plan to kill everyone you meet."

El Ojo del Gato

Learning to work with or "chase" for the night vision scope was critical. It was our bread and butter once nightfall came. Some of the senior agents used to say, "We rule the day, but the illegals rule the night." This was true, because the numbers of people crossing illegally at night was just overwhelming. The aliens referred to the scope as "el ojo del gato," or the eye of the cat. Actually, chasing for scope was a lot of fun, if not downright fascinating. Basically, the scope operator sees illegal traffic and the BP units go chase it.

In 1994, the scopes the Border Patrol had were a bit crude—by today's standards, anyway. Brown Field had two or three old military hand me downs called Tank Scopes. I assume that meant they had come from old army tanks, which is actually kinda cool. Once we got our hands on them, the scopes were usually adapted to fit inside the bed of some old pick-up truck that Border Patrol had seized from some drug dealer or human trafficker.

The pickup was usually junk, for the most part, and often could barely make it up the mountain. Once we reached a high point overlooking the target area, we first had to place rocks underneath the tires to keep our vehicle from rolling back down the mountain or over the edge of a cliff. Next, we would climb into the bed of the truck and place the very heavy scope on top of a metal pole that had been welded vertically into the center of the of the pickup bed floor. The pole stood up about three feet or so. The main body of the scope had a slightly larger diameter pipe affixed to the bottom side. This pipe slid down over the vertical pole on the truck. The larger pipe was shorter and had an arm with chair seat welded to it. Once we got it all put together, we could sit on the chair and swivel around the pole while looking through the scope. It was important, of course, to continually brace our feet against the inside of the truck bed, since we were usually parked on a sharp mountain incline. Otherwise, the chair and scope would violently swing downhill and the dizzy agent would see nothing but sky. So, this was quite a workout.

The scope itself was a thermal type, meaning it saw only heat signatures, but it was easy to identify whether a signal represented a person, cow, rabbit, car, etc. People looked more or less like diamonds or upright coffins, depending on how far away they were. The closer they were, the brighter they got. If someone walked directly in front of the scope at close range, the image would become so bright that it could actually do damage to the viewer's eyes.

The front ocular measured about four inches in diameter. At the opposite end of the scope was a small eyepiece. In order to see anything, we had to lean forward and put an eye directly onto the eyepiece to view a small lit screen inside. The screens could be either red or green, but the cameras were referred to as "redeye" scopes because the operator's eyes would be so red after using one, regardless of the screen color.

Some guys were really good at running these things, but since I had a slight astigmatism in my eyes, I was not. The first time I tried operating a scope, it was a disaster. The second time, I was only mildly horrible. After that, I was just so-so at it, and the station quickly learned not to put me on scope.

"Chasing" for a scope was a lot better than operating one—at least in my opinion. It is the ultimate exercise in communication and trust. Our safety, and sometimes our very lives, rested squarely in the scope operator's hands.

Since we did not normally use a flashlight during night operations, the scope operator would become the chasing agent's eyes. The "Chaser" is walking blind, while "Scope," as the operator is called, tells him or her every step to take—and I do mean every step.

A common transmission, for example, might sound like this: "Walk 200 yards straight south. Stop. Move forty yards to the southeast at a forty-five degree angle. Stop. Go ten feet hard east. Stop. Ok you're right on them."

Scope can identify how large a group is, can tell if they are armed, backpacking illegal drugs, setting up to ambush the agent, running away, and even whether or not an animal is creeping up from behind. If an agent on foot got jumped, Scope would call for backup, as a scrapping agent often cannot. In the event of trouble, the operator himself likely could not intervene on his partner's behalf, because he was usually two or three miles away, the scope, nonetheless, often saved our lives.

A Rock and a Hard Place

One night while I was still a NUG, I was assigned to the Otay Valley. In order to get down into the valley, it was necessary to pass through a several locked gates because a number of agents had previously been assaulted in the area.

Years earlier, this valley had been a favorite place for Mexican bandits to lie in wait for their prey. Bandits and smugglers like to refer to their cargo or victims (the illegals) as "pollos" (chickens), while the guide or smuggler was the "pollero" (chicken herder), so to speak.

This particular night I was working alone in the valley. The other agent assigned the valley that night was quite senior to me and, apparently, didn't care to work in the chosen area, so he never showed up. Nor did he bother passing that bit of information on to me or the Otay Valley Supervisor. He just went off to do his own thing, whatever that was.

Sometime around 2:00 in the morning, the scope operator spotted a single suspect walking the north side of Otay Valley. At the time, I was set up on the south side of the valley. As trainees we were taught to be very leery of singles, pairs, and small groups of three or four wandering around the valley or mountain. Almost always, these subjects turned out to have violent criminal histories. Large groups were often safer to work. Statistically, singles and pairs are responsible for most agent injuries and deaths.

As scope called the single out, I noticed that I was the only one that responded, and only then discovered that my assigned partner had not bothered to show up. The entire valley had been recently flooded and some of the normal crossings and paths were of little use. The solo alien was on the other side of the valley bottom, so there was little choice for me but to bail out and take off after him on foot. The valley was large, so it was a bit of a walk and took me several minutes to cross at the bottom.

It was very dark that night, and the going was slow, so Scope was continually giving me updates on the suspect's movements and making suggestions about which route was the best for me to take. Unfortunately, the valley bottom was littered with loose rock, making it was very hard to walk silently. As I closed in on the suspect, the scope operator suddenly called my star number with a note of urgency in his voice.

"Bravo 259, stop!"

Immediately, I went still. "What's up?" I inquired.

"The suspect is setting up to ambush you," he warned.

It appeared that the illegal had heard me crossing the rocks and was preparing to jump me. It was unclear whether or not he was armed, but he had stepped just off the trail and was waiting behind a small tree. The fact that he was standing was the indicator of the problem. Normally, an alien who is just trying to escape will dig in and hide underneath the nearest bush, so the behavior of this guy was concerning.

The scope operator had stopped me about 100 feet short of the ambush site.

"Scope, what's he doing?" I asked.

"He's just standing there, trying to find you."

That's not good, I thought. I gotta do something else. "Scope, can you put me in behind him?"

"Yeah, 10-4," he answered. "Go straight ahead fifty feet, make a hard right, there's a brush line that will take you right in behind him. It looks like dirt, so he shouldn't hear you."

"10-4," I replied and followed his instructions exactly. I entered behind the brush and could see nothing. It was extremely dark, but the ground was dirt and I could move silently toward my mark. Scope's instructions took me directly behind the man, within ten feet, in fact. My partner had done a beautiful job of guiding me in, but I still had no visual of the suspect. Scope assured me that I was indeed right behind him and in a very good position to take him down. I was also now close enough to use a flashlight and draw a weapon.

I lit up my flashlight and aimed my revolver on his back. Sure enough, he had no clue that I was that close, much less right behind him, and was still looking down the trail where he had last heard me. In my best Spanish, I said something like, "Ensename los manos, o desparo" (Show me your hands or I'll shoot).

The suspect dropped a large, three-pound rock that he had been clutching and slowly raised his now empty hands.

I always made it a habit never to cuff standing suspects, because if something went wrong, nobody could get to me in time to help. So, I put him on the ground. After the man was lying face down in the dirt with both hands behind his back, I cuffed and searched him, very aware that we still had about a half of a mile of valley bottom to cross together. Such a long walk can also be dangerous, since it gives the suspect ample opportunity to think up a Plan B. I made sure my suspect understood well that any Plan B would turn out much worse for him than Plan A had, so our twenty-minute stroll back to the truck was an uneventful one.

After finally getting mobile, I met with transport and turned over the 10-15. About an hour later, the station called and advised me to report to processing because I had a case to write up. Sure enough, the alien was a career criminal who had done hard time for armed robbery and assault with a deadly weapon. Rightfully, this man was headed right back to prison.

A Dangerous Occupation

Now, working the scope itself could also be a dangerous occupation. While sitting in the bed of an uncovered pickup, the scope operator was completely exposed not only to the elements but also to the smugglers and aliens. The scope when in use also made a continuous clicking sound that kept the operator from being able to detect subtle sounds around the truck, like footsteps.

Also, after looking through the thermal for so long, the agent would lose the ability to see without the device and, for several minutes, would be almost completely blind. If someone quietly approached the scope operator while he was concentrating on a group, he might never know it. Therefore, as a tactic, if the bad guys wanted to move a large load of contraband, they might plan to attack the scope operator first and then proceed with the operation. Some areas, in fact, were so dangerous for an operator that a second agent would be sent to guard the scope operator's back. However, most agents had no backup and operated the equipment alone.

Over the years, several scope operators were assaulted while running the device. For this reason, an agent on foot is taught from day one to never approach the scope position without first making positive contact with the operator on the radio.

One night, I was running the scope from a position atop the mountain in a high traffic area. All other agents had been ordered off the mountain because of impending weather, so I was the sole PA left on the mountain that night. A couple of bored East Mesa units thought it would be funny to quietly ride their ATVs into my area.

They parked their quads and hiked up into a position behind me. Of course, I did not hear them. The clicking of the scope was louder than their footsteps, and I had no natural night vision left after peering so long through the redeye. One of them let out a scream as the two approached. I instinctively spun around and drew a firearm. They were not too pleased that I had drawn on them, but what did they expect? Seriously!

A few months later, another agent and I were assigned the Otay Valley on a midnight shift. Around two or three in the morning, scope spotted a single alien walking westbound in the bottom of the valley. My partner Roy and I were already out on foot and just west of the suspect, so we started walking eastbound and asked the scope operator to guide us in. Within a few minutes, Scope had walked us within seventy yards of our target. As we got closer, we slowed down and moved with more purpose, so to speak, because we didn't want the alien to hear us and then bust and run.

Finally, Scope had us within thirty feet of the suspect and we were preparing to pounce when we discovered we were apparently not the only ones stalking the alien.

We were moving in when the scope operator, suddenly rather excited, radioed in. "10-3, 10-3! Hold up a sec!"

We stopped.

"The alien is only twenty feet away," he explained, "but a mountain lion just walked between you. He's sizing up the alien and—wait...now he's looking at you!"

All the while, Roy and I could see nothing but darkness. We reached for our flashlights to scare the cat off or, at least, see it before it attacked.

Before we could light up, Scope came back and said, "The alien just took off running...and there goes the cat!"

Running was the worst thing the illegal could have done. When something runs from a cat, its killer instinct kicks off and the chase is on. At this point, the alien was on borrowed time. There was no way he could outrun the animal.

Roy and I were still in the danger zone as well, and we knew it. We quickly turned on our lights and searched the area for the animal, but found the alien instead. It was his lucky night. All the commotion and lights had startled the wild feline and, fortunately, discouraged it from attacking.

"The cat just took off," said Scope. "I can't see it anymore."

That news was both good and bad. The cat was no longer in our immediate area, which was good, but we didn't know where it had gone either.

Roy and I never caught even the slightest glimpse of the animal that night, but, once again, the scope had saved our lives.

Chapter 6
Otay Mesa
Beware of the Flats

S itting at the base of Otay Mountain is a four and a half mile stretch of land, which is home to the ten-foot high fence separating the United States from Mexico. We lovingly referred to it as the "East Mesa." This, of course, implies that a "West Mesa" exists as well, and it does. The West Mesa was a place of legend and great terror to those who crossed into it. Both the east and west mesas sat against the border fence, and were separated by the Otay Mesa Port of Entry (POE) and State Route 905.

There have been books and even movies that have chronicled the events of West Mesa in places known as The Soccer Field, Spring and Dillon, Huarache Flats, and the dreaded Ambush Alley. We briefly worked the west side when I first arrived at Brown Field, and then passed the torch to the Chula Vista Station as our focus shifted to the Otay Mountain Range. The

51

West Mesa had been and continues to be a place where very bad things could happen very quickly.

When I arrived in 1994, there was no lighting anywhere along the border fence on the East Mesa side. Every agent knew, and knew well, the most dangerous area of operations was the border fence itself. It's ugly there.

Brown Field's current section of border fence started at the Otay Mesa Port of Entry and ran east all the way to the base of Otay Mountain and then ended at a place called the "Well Draw." A draw is basically a valley between ridgelines of a mountain. This area got its name because there was an old well in the bottom of the draw. It was also called the "End of Fence," because that's where the border fence ended. You see, that's how we name things in the Border Patrol. Everything is either painfully obvious or entirely self-explanatory. If some PA happened to see a dead cow in a certain canyon, then that location was rightfully named "Dead Cow Canyon." If another agent once found a coffee cup on a trail, this trail was henceforth and forevermore known as "Coffee Cup Trail."

See how it works? Very simple. And, lest you think I'm joking, let me assure that these are, in fact, the official names of those areas. Typically, some Border Patrol agent who had retired fifty years before was responsible for the names of these locations, but the titles stuck! As funny as some of these names are, however, if an agent got caught in one of the notorious regions after dark without backup, laughter was the last thing on his or her mind.

So, let's take a little tour of the mesa. The U.S. side of the mesa was barren and uninhabited, while on the Mexican side to the south, there were thousands of wooden pallet homes and cardboard shacks. Three miles to the east of the Otay Mesa Port of Entry is Tin Can Hill, while Johnny Wolf's Draw sits at the west base of Tin Can Hill. Running from south to north, Johnny Wolf's is the first passageway leading up to Otay Mountain and that promised pathway to citizenship. A mile and a half further to the east, Tin Can is the End of Fence and the Well Draw.

When I was a NUG, the Well Draw and Tin Can areas were manned only during daylight hours and only by NUGs because these were such dreaded positions. The senior guys had paid their dues, so now it was the New Ugly Guy's turn to earn his keep by taking the more undesirable assignments. When working the evening or swing shifts, a supervisor would give us very specific instructions on how to work the area.

Something like: "Once it gets dark, get the %$#! out of there."

I tried to always heed such good advice because, once the sun went down, there was always gunfire in the shack town on the Mexico side of the East Mesa. Of the approximately 398 times I ventured east of Johnny Wolf's Draw after dark, I heard gunfire exactly 398 times!

Other useful advice was: "Never go into the Well Draw alone. Always go with at least three or four or seven other PAs."

From what I understand, there were some rather notorious shootouts down in the Well Draw in previous years. It was no secret that any PA hanging around Johnny Wolf's Draw, Tin Can Hill, or near the End of Fence after dark would be shot at and likely return with an assortment of bullet holes in his Bronco. It was important for the units assigned those areas to avoid that because then he would have to write a memo. And writing memos was worse than getting shot at! Trust me. I know. I was shot at. Then, a few days later, my vehicle partner brought our brand new Ford Bronco back to the station with a fresh bullet hole in the front fender—a trophy for his little excursion east of Johnny Wolf's after dark. Maybe somebody should have run a red flag up a pole to let us know the firing range was hot!

Johnny Wolf's Draw

Johnny Wolf's Draw was named in honor of the American Indian man who had once lived there. I never met Mr. Wolf personally; his untimely death occurred before I joined the Patrol. However, according to the agents who knew him, he was somewhat of a legend.

Mr Wolf had continual confrontations with the smugglers who constantly crossed his land, destroyed his property, and caused every kind of trouble. He grew to hate them—all of them—and many of these confrontations ended in gunfire.

An older agent once told me, "Every time Johnny killed a smuggler, he would bury him just north of his house and plant a pepper tree on top of him."

I have no way of knowing whether this is true or just folklore, but I can tell you that just north of Johnny's old house there are quite a few pepper trees all planted in a perfect row. Oddly enough, the grass seems to be just a little greener around each one.

One night a group of smugglers finally got the drop on him. The bandits snuck into Johnny Wolf's house and murdered him while he slept in his bed. The old rock house this man once called home has since fallen down and now lies in ruin, but his legend remains.

Tin Can Hill

A BP unit parked on top of Tin Can Hill could control and direct his fellow agents to all parts of the East Mesa as well as monitor drive-throughs. A drive-through occurred when drug smugglers would cut a hole in the fence with a cutting torch from the south side, drive a truck loaded with a thousand pounds of marijuana through the hole, and then race the PAs to the promised land.

The smugglers knew that Tin Can Hill was critical, and their name for the hill was "Nido de las aguilas"(The eagle's nest). Sometimes, these drug runners would go to great lengths to get the agent off Tin Can Hill if he was up there after dark. As you will soon see.

As mentioned previously, there were some things we just knew not to do, and sitting on Tin Can Hill after dark was one of them.

When I was fresh off the training unit and had been on my own for several months, I remember having fun in the field and enjoying my late shift. I liked working at night. Most of us did; however, Janet Reno came to visit our station and changed all that.

Operation Gatekeeper started in 1994 at the Imperial Beach Station, and it was a disaster. The operation consisted mainly of parking a non-bulletproof Border Patrol vehicle next to the border fence and just sitting at a stationary location, marked by an imaginary X, without moving for an entire shift. At night, we were expected to sit there with our headlights on so the aliens could see where we were. The aliens, of course, would be so "terrified" that they wouldn't even think about crossing.

Perhaps in some areas along the fence this tactic could work to some degree, but only if there are sufficient back up units to fill in the gaps after the aliens get past the X-sitting scarecrows.

Sometimes we didn't have that kind of back-up.

So one day Attorney General Janet Reno came to the Brown Field Station and told us we should sit on an X all night at places like Tin Can Hill and the End of the Fence. And, just to be certain we did, she was going to fly over the East Mesa later that night, at a time known only to her, and look out the helicopter window to see us all sitting there with our lights on.

Brilliant!

Of course, I had the good fortune to be a NUG working the evening shift; so, guess who strapped a target on his chest and drew Tin Can Hill as his assignment for the night?

Yeah team!

All went well too…until it got dark. Funny how things change once the sun goes down. It was actually quite a pleasant evening prior to that, and I sat there with the windows down, enjoying the cool evening air. It was a Saturday night, and I was listening to the Oklahoma vs. Colorado football game on the radio. I almost forgot what a crappy and dangerous assignment I had embarked on.

Now, on the Mexican side just south of Tin Can, there was a very large radio antenna standing among all the cardboard shacks. Guess who put that up?

Around 9:30 p.m., an unknown voice broke into the main Brown Field radio frequency and announced there would be a drive through attempt between the Eagle's Nest and the End of the Fence around 10:00 p.m. The man spoke in English and without an accent, but he referred to Tin Can Hill by its Mexican name the Eagle's Nest. The individual did not identify himself, but he certainly wasn't one of our guys in green. True, it is possible he could have been an undercover agent with another agency, but we doubted that. More likely, it was one group of smugglers offering up info on another group hoping to stop the opposing shipment from getting through. Or, it could have been a rouse prompting us to reinforce that area and let our guard down somewhere else where the real drive through attempt would be made.

How the voice forced its way on to our frequency is not clear, but that big ol' antenna standing amongst all those cardboard shacks was looking rather tall and useful. I had heard our radio traffic echoing back to us from the shacks next to that antenna before. Our radios were not encrypted at that time, and it was common knowledge that smugglers monitored our radio traffic at all times.

A few moments after receiving the information, the agent sitting at the end of the fence reported seeing someone with a cutting torch carving a hole into the border fence on the Mexican side between his position and mine. Seconds later, I heard several long bursts of automatic rifle fire from an AK-47 originating on top of Tin Can Hill, but still south of the fence. I could not see the muzzle flash, or tell where the rounds were hitting, but the shots sounded very close. Immediately, the agent at the End of Fence reported shots fired in the Well Draw next to his position.

Almost as fast as the shots were reported over the radio, a supervisor broadcast over the air that we were not to leave our positions because the Attorney General hadn't flown over to see us yet and, when she did, we had better be there or else. Well, God forbid I move my Bronco to a safer location away from the automatic gunfire raining down on me, thereby depriving Her Majesty of her fly-over fairytale.

Certainly, these weren't real bullets anyway, because guns are outlawed in Mexico, which meant these probably weren't real weapons firing at us either.

So far, the shots were only meant to just scare us off our X's, but clearly indicated, if we didn't leave, that could change. Our problem was that the bad

Figure 1—On top of Tin Can Hill looking east towards the "End of Fence."

Figure 2—Overlooking Johnny Wolf's Draw west to the Otay POE, from Tin Can Hill.

57

guys could see us quite easily, aim at their leisure, and take a shot anytime they chose, but we couldn't see them at all due to the handy solid metal border fence they were hiding behind. Not to mention, every few feet there were convenient little holes in the fence panels just big enough to stick a rifle barrel through, allowing the shooters to remain entirely protected from incoming fire. We, on the other hand, were sitting ducks.

And where was that politician and my supervisor? Good question, because they certainly weren't on top of Tin Can Hill with me!

Well, I wasn't going to sit there like some kind of an idiot and wait to be shot for anybody, supervisor or politician, just because they told me to. I left the headlights on and the vehicle running just like my supervisor instructed, but then climbed out of the Bronco and left it there. I crept back to a pile of large rocks behind my vehicle's position and took cover there. With my headlights shining in their eyes, I knew the shooters couldn't tell I had left the vehicle. From this vantage point, I had a much better chance of seeing them than they had of seeing me. I also had a twelve-gauge shotgun loaded with slugs that could tear through that border fence like hot butter.

A few more tense moments passed, but then the smugglers chose to reschedule their fun and called off the drive-through. In the end, it was much ado about nothing, but I gained some experience and learned a valuable lesson. A truck is never adequate "cover" in a gunfight. How many officers have been gunned down while crouching behind their police cruisers, thinking they were safe? Far too many.

God save us from politicians with brilliant ideas.

Coker Strikes Again!

Janet's helicopter ride fiasco ended and things went back to normal on the East Mesa, at least for a while. NUGs were manning the worst X's until dark and then getting out of there as fast as they could. The End of Fence had an exceptionally dangerous X because of how the agent was required to get into and then back out of position. Unlike other X positions, the End of Fence could only be accessed from one direction. In order to get to that particular spot, the agent had to drive the border road right up next to the fence for about a half of mile or so. After arriving at the end of the border fence, the PA then drove north up the ridgeline alongside the Well Draw. These roads were very rough and slow going, which left plenty of time for bad guys to throw rocks or shoot their weapons from the Mexican side of the border. This section of our area, specifically, was where the really, really bad guys liked to hang out.

To make matters worse, the radio communications at the End of Fence/Well Draw area was almost non-existent. An agent could communicate with the Tin Can position and that was about it. Worst part of all, once a PA was set in position, there was no way to escape. In order to leave the area, the agent had to slowly negotiate the road back down towards the border, which is exactly where the attack would be coming from in the first place. Most PAs planned to simply leave their vehicles where they were and make a run for cover on foot if attacked at that position.

We used to joke, "If you get killed there at the beginning of a shift, no one would know until the end of shift eight hours later." And that was true. Nobody ever came to check on that position, nor could most agents with that assignment communicate on their radios. As soon as we had to start manning the End of Fence around the clock, it was the one place that a wise agent would never allow himself to fall prey to the need for a nap, otherwise known as the Z Monster. This was a serious place to be, and a sleeping agent could wake up dead real quick. When I was assigned that spot on midnight shift, I would do anything to stay awake. No matter how tired I was, dozing off was not an option. I would do jumping jacks, pushups, wind sprints—whatever it took to stay awake.

A few days after the Attorney General concluded her visit to our fine station, I was assigned the horrid End of Fence position and my buddy "Captain America" was assigned Tin Can Hill. For now, the strategy for the two eastern X's was back to normal: Sit there until dark, and then get the %$#! out of there.

Captain America had picked up the nickname from some of his Academy classmates. He had been a Captain in the army, was fiercely patriotic, and had a very good, though dry, sense of humor. This man was easily one of my favorite people to work with. With him, there was never a dull moment.

Our shift started out uneventful enough, but then came sundown. Almost immediately, four armed bandits showed up at the End of Fence. A few days earlier a Mexican Officer had been killed by bandits at the end of the fence just south of my location, and I was aware of it. Right away, these guys started trying to intimidate me. I have to admit they were rather successful. I was armed only with a single revolver and had no avenue of escape.

I had attempted to check out a shotgun at the beginning of shift, but the Duty Supervisor had foolishly talked me out of it. "You don't need it," he assured. "Nothing is going to happen."

Upon seeing the bandits, I put out a call on the radio for backup, but no one answered. I tried to call dispatch, but again the call fell on deaf ears. I was in a dead spot, meaning radio communications were not possible at my current location. Nobody heard my calls for assistance and no one was coming my way. Since our vehicles were considered to be more coffin than cover, the only thing I could think of was to leave the vehicle and grab the high ground while I had the chance. I did just that. Fortunately, my actions discouraged the bandits and they retreated south back into Mexico. By then, it was nearly dark. I quickly got back to my ride and left the area.

Never again did I let anyone talk me out of taking an extra weapon when I wanted it.

After that, I met up with Captain America and told him about the incident, then asked him if he had a shotgun.

"No," he said, "they didn't give me one either."

Just as the Captain and I started formulating a plan on how to deal with the bandit situation, a sudden scream blasted over the radio. This was a long, drawn out scream that faded gently into the night air, easily worthy of an opera singer.

"Well Drawww!" it shrieked.

What followed was total silence.

"No one should be in the Well Draw," I said. "Unless one of the mountain guys came down into it from the top and ran into those bandits."

Captain America asked over the radio, "Is there an agent requiring assistance in the Well Draw?"

There was no answer. A supervisor then came over the air, clearly excited, and demanded, "Everybody get to the Well Draw. Find out what's going on."

By everybody, he meant the Captain and me, since there were no others close by. So, the two of us charged blindly into the Well Draw at the end of the fence without knowing what to expect or who was involved. We entered the draw as tactically as we could, ready for anything, and immediately ran into about twenty-five aliens. None of them seemed to be armed, however, and there was no sign of any distressed agent. The group of aliens TBS'd (Turned Back South), but we did not pursue. Our only objective at that time was to find the agent in need and nothing else.

By the time we started making our way up the draw towards the top of the mountain, the helicopter, whose call sign was Foxtrot, arrived. Normally, he did not fly on the mountain after dark, but this was an emergency concerning officer safety, though nothing further had been heard from the agent or agents in distress. Rather quickly, Foxtrot located the agent in need.

It was Agent Coker.

There was no emergency. Coker and two other PAs were merely working a large group of aliens when he became overly excited and screamed out his position. The illegals were running back down the Well Draw and he wanted someone to help corral them in. About that same time, the Captain and I met with a wall of humanity. About a hundred or so illegals were running amuck in the draw and heading right for us. We took about twenty of them down right off the bat, but the guide got away. During the melee, my flashlight was somehow destroyed. Coker and his group took about fifty suspects, and we rounded up another fifteen. Captain America even managed to run down the guide who originally eluded us.

We eventually walked out of Well Draw with eighty-five prisoners in tow, yet the supervisor and his boss, the Field Operations Supervisor, were far from pleased.

They were furious!

Coker and his dramatics had caused every agent on Otay Mesa, and even parts of the Valley, to leave their assigned position and rush towards the Well Draw. For that, Coker got the kind of butt chewing that only a Border Patrol Supervisor can give!

That is what we commonly referred to as a "Coker Moment!"

Fate or Flashlight

The next day, I went to see about replacing my flashlight. I gave my broken light to the supply officer and waited while he searched for a replacement.

A moment later, he returned and handed me one. "Here. This is used," he said, "but it's the last one."

The flashlight had a star number etched in its side—B282—a number I recognized. I handed it back. "Not this one. I don't feel comfortable with this light," I told him.

"Why not?"

"It's Luis Santiago's light. It was assigned to him when he was killed."

"It's all we got," replied the supply officer, "take it or leave it."

I took it, though reluctantly, and carried it throughout the rest of my career. When I retired years later and was turning in my equipment, I asked if I could keep it. I still have the flashlight to this day. It was eerie how things concerning Santiago's death kept coming back to me. In fact, he was one of the reasons I felt so compelled to write this book.

Chapter 7
Otay Mountain
The Forbidden Passage

S ome of my most memorable shifts occurred in the Otay Mountains. These mysterious but unassuming mountains start at about sea level and rise up to about 3,650 feet. These mountains are considered sacred by the local Kumeyaay Indian tribe. They say it is forbidden for human beings to go up there for fear of invoking evil spirits and ancient curses.

Or so I was told.

Indeed, the entire Otay Mountain range is pretty much off limits. As it is Bureau of Land Management (BLM) property, a few folks will drive up to the top and back when necessary, but nobody is allowed to live or stay there, so the range is completely uninhabited. Even BLM officials themselves seldom go into the area. It is the roughest terrain I have ever seen or traversed in my life.

Most parts of this small but brutal range are impassible, even on horseback, and must be worked solely on foot. There is but a narrow, single lane dirt road that travels up its spine, running about twenty miles from east to west.

The "Minnewawa" Truck Trail runs north and south, connecting Otay Lakes Road to the Otay Truck Trail. The Minnewawa was an exceptionally treacherous road in some places. In some areas of the Minnewawa, it is entirely possible to plunge 1500 feet or more over an edge. In fact, when I first arrived at the Brown Field Station, the road was impassable even in four-wheel drive and was closed to all traffic, although it was reopened shortly thereafter.

These two roads give Border Patrol Agents access to the mountain range. A vehicle was definitely the fastest way to cover ground on top and move from canyon to canyon, but we could not actually work from a vehicle. Virtually all patrols and apprehensions occurred while working on foot.

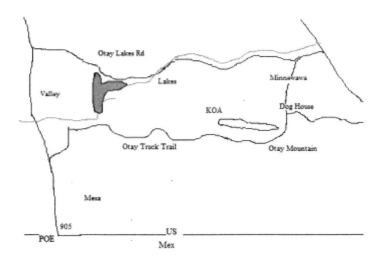

Otay Mountain is the kind of place that can break hard men. It had taken the lives of countless illegal aliens, airplane and helicopter pilots and crews, ten members of country music legend Reba McEntire's band and flight crew, and several Border Patrol Agents. Whether or not it is sacred ground I cannot say, but a person either respects the area or loses his life.

As beautiful as the mountains are, I could always feel the ever-constant presence of evil, sadness, and horror that has played out there time and time again. Virtually no wildlife live up there, save a few rattlesnakes and a handful of mountain lions, so there is continual and absolute silence throughout both ranges. It is so quiet, in fact, that one can sometimes hear people talking in Mexico despite standing on top of the mountain two miles away.

The Otay and Tecate Mountains physically look alike and are separated by Marron Valley, which runs north and south all the way from Highway 94 to the Mexican border. Its bottom is barely twenty feet wide in places, and there is a single lane dirt road leading all the way south to the border.

Marron Valley has its own troubled past. Except for Dam Canyon, it is the darkest place at night that I have ever seen. One night, I stepped out of a solid white Ford Bronco no more than two or three feet for a quick nature call but once I got out, I could no longer see the vehicle. Its walls are steep, often leaving the entire valley totally devoid of any light after sunset. One could envision the kind of place that would invoke the biblical words of, "Yeah, though I walk through the valley of the shadow of death . . ."

That is Marron Valley.

Doghouse Junction sits at the peak of Otay Mountain. At the top is where the Minnewawa runs north and meets up with the Otay Truck Trail. This is also where the plane carrying Reba McEntire's band crashed, killing everyone on board. The crash actually occurred a year or two before I entered into the Patrol, but there was a large amount of debris still in the area when I arrived.

Border Patrol agents actually witnessed the fireball from that crash and were the first to respond to the scene. The agents even put up a small shrine at the site as a memorial. Although a fire in 1996 swept the mountain, the stones of the memorial remain.

The entire event was such a needless tragedy. Had the plane been twenty-five feet higher or forty feet to the left or right, it would have cleared the peak, and they would have lived to see another day.

I must admit, I was never a diehard country music fan, but Reba McEntire was a fellow Oklahoman and I had several of her albums. She was by far my favorite country singer. I first saw her perform at the National Finals Rodeo when it was still in Oklahoma City in the mid-1970s. She sang the National Anthem, and it was best rendition of the Star Spangled Banner I have ever heard. Actually, I believe that was her debut.

I thought it was rather ironic that her band's plane crashed inside of my work area. Of the paranormal activity that I will tell you about later, however, none of it seems to concern this tragic plane crash…except for one event.

Miguel, a fellow agent who had been on duty at the time of the accident and who had been part of the recovery effort, told me of an unusual occurrence that happened to him a few years later.

About two years after the crash, Miguel and his partner had parked their truck near the crash site and took off on a short hike after dark to lay-in for some traffic expected to arrive out of Copper Canyon. The traffic never arrived, so, after a while, they started back toward their vehicle.

About 150 yards out, they noticed the lights on their Bronco blinking and flashing and thought someone was trying to break into the vehicle, so they ran to it as fast as they could. Upon arriving, however, they discovered that the truck had not been tampered with. The Agents started cutting for tracks leading up to or away from the truck, but there were none. This was in 1994, long before any of our trucks were equipped with remote-start keys that could activate lights or door locks.

Miguel wasn't claiming that it was paranormal for certain, but he thought it very strange, as he had never seen anything like that happen before. Other than this one account, in the thirteen years I was at Brown Field, I never heard any agent claim to experience paranormal activity at that crash site. May their spirits all rest in peace.

At times, the mountain felt completely surreal. It seemed like things could occur up there that the laws of the universe do not allow anywhere else. Throughout the years, there have been several airplane crashes near Doghouse Junction. For the most part, these went down well below the peak around Copper or Windmill Canyons.

Copper Canyon was a monster of a canyon to hike through and to work around. It started at the border fence with Mexico and ran north about four miles or so. Starting at sea level, it peaked out at Dog House around 3,650 feet. Any agent venturing down into Copper is wise to be prepared for anything. If trouble happened down there, rescue efforts would likely be futile. Yet, PAs frequently went into the canyon and brought out huge groups all the time.

One day early in the morning, my partner B271 and I went down into Copper Canyon. When we reached the bottom, we caught about twenty illegals, all male and all in their twenties. While we were there, an agent in an adjacent canyon called for assistance. No emergency, he just needed help working some traffic. My partner took off cross-country to help, while I stayed back with the prisoners.

So, I had to walk the group back up the canyon wall alone—2,000 feet in elevation back to the top where our vehicles were parked—and I had twenty unwilling participants in tow. There were certain tactics we used back then to discourage aliens from trying to jump agents or run away, but those won't be discussed here. We have to keep some secrets. Nevertheless, four hours later we reached the top, and I still had all twenty prisoners. The climb back to the top was rather steep, and I was a little surprised that I had kept them all together for so long in such difficult terrain.

The Headless Hiker

When I was a NUG and still on the field training unit, there was a murder committed up on the KOA ridgeline. It was jokingly named the KOA in reference to the "Kampgrounds Of America."

The ridgeline sat between the Otay Truck Trail on the mountain and Otay Lakes Road, but ran parallel to both. The ridgeline sat up high, so the guides and smugglers could easily watch for Border Patrol agents coming into both areas, day or night. There were no roads leading up to the ridgeline, and it was very difficult for agents to access it without being seen. Around 2,000 feet up, it could only be accessed on foot and was a monster to hike because of the climb. The guides could easily see anyone trying to hike up and would just run down the other side of the ridgeline long before the first PA ever got to the top. The best way to work the KOA, therefore, was from the north side by patiently waiting for the illegals to come down towards Otay Lake where they would hopefully be seen by the scope.

Management tried to play the killing off as no big deal and refused to even admit it was a murder. They said it could have been caused by some kind of accident or even natural causes, except that…the head was missing and the Sheriff's Department had arrived to look for it.

"Yeah right," echoed the agents who had been to the scene. "A machete accidentally took her head off."

The machete must have accidentally walked away with it, too, because they never found the woman's head, nor did they ever learn who did it or why. Notice was served. This was the kind of crime that one could expect to encounter on that beautiful mountaintop. So, yes, Virginia, the bogeyman is real, and he lives on Otay Mountain!

Don't Worry About It

At the peak of Otay Mountain, there were several antennas and a small maintenance building, and many different law enforcement agencies used them. One night, about midnight, Rich and I noticed a light at one of the maintenance sheds. Just a few days earlier, I had taken down a bandit very near the area so we decided to investigate.

When Rich and I pulled up to the shed we saw a pickup parked outside and figured it was a radio technician. We went inside and struck up a conversation with the tech. I believe he said he was a Drug Enforcement Agent or perhaps the Alcohol Tobacco and Firearms. I am writing this from memory of more than eighteen years, so I am not one hundred percent certain which agency he was with. Nevertheless, we talked for a while before I noticed he did not appear to be armed. I asked him if he had a gun.

"Oh sure," he said, "it's out in the pickup."

I told him there had been bandits in the area recently and that if something happened and he really needed his weapon, he would probably never make it to his pickup. The agent thanked me for my concern, but said he wasn't worried about it. He had been coming up there at night for a fair amount of time and had never had a problem. He wasn't Border Patrol, he said, so why would someone want to mess with him? We talked for a while longer and then bid the man goodnight.

A night or two later, I was working Doghouse Junction again, this time with a trainee whose name I have since forgotten. Again, I noticed somebody at the maintenance shed. This time, however, I was working traffic and did not have time to stop and visit.

About 11:00 p.m., a rare but fierce rainstorm swept across Otay Mountain, prompting the supervisors to call all the agents off the mountain. The rain and wind were so bad that we had to stop several times on the way down because we couldn't see to drive. Finally, we made the uneventful trip back to the station.

The next night during our pre-shift muster briefing, a supervisor asked if anyone had seen anything unusual at Doghouse Junction the night before. Specifically, had anyone witnessed anything near the antennas or the maintenance building? I told him my partner and I had been up there until about eleven o'clock the night before, but saw nothing amiss.

"Why do you ask?" I wondered.

The supervisor replied that about midnight a bandit had attacked a DEA agent or employee working at the antennas. The man had been stabbed around fourteen times and was in critical condition. They suspected that after we pulled off the mountain, the bandit had spotted the building's light and headed for it. The bandit caught the unsuspecting agent off guard, robbed him, and then stabbed him repeatedly.

The supervisor didn't tell us, though, how the employee was rescued. Whether it was the same agent I spoke with a few nights earlier or not, I do not know. I was always amazed at the people who thought they were safe up on the mountain and refused to heed the warnings issued by the Border Patrol agents who worked there continuously.

Rape Trees

The very first time I ever hiked down a trail on the mountain, I immediately noticed there were women's panties lying around all over the place—on the trails, in the bushes, the trees. At first, it caught me off guard. Why would women stop and change their clothes on the trail and leave their panties behind? I did not realize the significance of it at first, but then it hit me. These were all rape victims.

I was stunned at how many there were. It was impossible to walk down any trail anywhere on the mountain and not see women's panties thrown all over the place. I learned later from some senior agents that the smugglers and polleros held contests between themselves to see who could rape the most women. They blatantly displayed their panties on the trails and trees as proof.

I came to realize early on in my career that every foot guide on the mountain was a rapist and a murderer as these men often left people who could not keep up behind to die. Other times, they would kill one or some of the aliens, themselves, for whatever reason. They sometimes even led their groups directly to waiting bandits for a cut of the loot.

It was quite disgusting.

The guide would make up an excuse to leave the group for a few minutes. Saying something like, "Wait here while I scout the trail up ahead." Then his bandit friends would move in to prey upon the group of pollos—raping, robbing, and murdering, whatever they felt like doing, for as long as they felt like doing it.

When it was over, the guide would return and pretend to know nothing about what had just taken place. Mountain guides ruled their groups with intimidation and violence. They were anything but the folk heroes the movies and news media would like you to believe.

Pushing groups over the mountain was physically draining, and foot guides often needed to push more than one group a week to make money. In order to do that, they usually doped up—crystal meth seemed to be their drug of choice. After a while, their brains just burned out. Often, it was easy to spot the guides because they were the ones with the dead, expressionless eyes. We were really dealing with something that was almost subhuman. At that point, they were truly zombies.

Knowing this helped me play it extra safe. I was very aware that when I was up on the mountain, it was a whole different game. Every time I confronted a group of aliens alone up there, my gun was in my hand, especially if it was during hours of darkness. I did this not to intimidate them, but to protect myself in case the group turned on me. I usually didn't point it at them, I merely held it alongside my leg just out of sight, mostly because I didn't want them to know where it was.

As previously mentioned, a common alien maneuver was to try and disarm the agent, but I stayed ready for that one. If someone jumped me and went for the gun he thought was in the holster, it would not be there. The weapon was much easier to protect that way. Many agents used the same tactic. A rifle or shotgun is always carried in the hand and nothing is thought of it, but carrying a pistol in the hand tends to sound paranoid. It isn't. Let me tell you what happened to Bravo 271, a fellow PA and friend of mine.

Attack on Bravo 271

It was just another typical midnight shift, and B271 and several other mountain units were working a group of about fifteen illegal aliens up on the mountain. B271 got separated from the other PAs after they had spread out to cover more ground.

A short time later, B271 ran into a group of illegals on his own, but these were standing. As he approached, the group suddenly rushed him. Five suspects jumped him and went straight for his sidearm, which was holstered.

Fortunately, B271's hand had locked around the grip. As the gun slid out, B271 pulled the trigger and held it down, firing off one shot. This action saved his life for two reasons: First, it sent a warning to his partners that he needed help, and fast. Secondly, it kept the trigger from cycling again, which would have meant his death.

During the fight, all five illegals were beating and kicking him. After the shot fired, they managed to stick the gun underneath his chin and tried to pull the trigger again, but the agent was still holding the trigger down to keep it from resetting. While this was happening, one of the illegal scumbags wrapped B271's radio microphone cord around his neck and tried to choke him to death with it while the others were busy biting him.

Help arrived in time to save this agent's life, and my friend survived his ordeal. However, if Bravo 271 had truly been working alone, as BP agents often did, he would not have lived to tell about it.

When working alone on the mountain after dark and confronting multiple suspects, the best place for the gun is in the hand.

El Diablo

Early in my career, I was assigned to work Doghouse Junction with three other agents—Brett, Manny, and John—due to the massive amounts of traffic that had been crossing through the area on the midnight shift. The four of us drove up the backside of the mountain on the Minnewawa and parked before we reached the top because we did not want the pollos and polleros to see our headlights coming up. We hiked up the rest of the way to Doghouse Junction and then headed south on the road from there.

We only made it a few hundred yards when we bumped head on into a group of about thirty illegals. We caught about twenty of them, but the rest jumped off the road and ran down into Copper Canyon.

John took off after the runners while the rest of us dealt with the twenty in custody. We needed to hide the 10-15s quickly and set back up before the next wave of aliens arrived, so we took them up a little hill and hid them in the brush. We didn't want to take prisoners back to where we parked and wait for transport every time we caught someone because that would give away our position and ruin any chance we had at catching larger groups later in the shift. So, we had to babysit them for a few hours.

After we got the twenty hidden from sight, Manny stayed behind to guard them. He was up higher on the hill and in a good spot to watch the road with his binoculars, so he could call out the traffic before it got to us. As my partner Brett and I began walking back to the road to set up again, Manny spotted another group of thirty coming right at us.

But, we were not ready!

Brett and I had not yet made it all the way back to our positions, so we had no choice but to sit down right where we were and try our best to look like bushes.

We had no more sat down when Manny called out another bunch of thirty behind the first. Then, he told us he could see thirty more behind that!

And they just kept coming.

Manny stopped trying to count them all when he reached a soft count of 130 illegals heading right for us. Even if my partner and I had gotten properly set up, there was still only two of us to bust all of them. John was still down below in the canyon, and Manny was guarding twenty prisoners up the hill.

About that time, John called on the radio to tell us he caught three or four of the suspects he had been chasing and said one of the guys he had in custody was a foot guide who had given us a warning. "One of the smugglers leading groups coming up the mountain is known as 'El Diablo' (the Devil), a very bad hombre (man)," he said. "Suspect is wearing a dark green t-shirt."

As the massive group approached our position, we hastily tried to put a plan together. With our radio mics right next to our ears and by speaking very softly, we were able to communicate with each other without alerting the groups.

As the first group of aliens got near, I would make a coughing sound, which would cause the guide to freeze for a moment. While the smuggler tried to figure out where I was, Manny would talk to him from the hillside, since he was the only one fluent in Spanish.

That was the plan.

So, the group came up. I coughed, and the guide stopped. When he stopped, he stopped not only his group, but all the groups behind him as well. This guy was definitely the one in charge. We could plainly see the man now, and he was indeed wearing a dark green t-shirt. Surely, this was "El Diablo."

El Diablo stood there a moment before he saw me sitting on the hill slightly above him.

For several moments, he just stared at me, clearly trying to decide what to do. Then Manny called out from the hillside and told him we were lost and wanted to join his group. At this news, El Diablo started pacing back and forth just below me, getting slightly closer with each new round.

Well, I wasn't stupid. I had long since drawn my pistol. Brett was lying on the ground behind me and had also drawn his weapon. We had no way of knowing yet if this El Diablo character was armed or what he might try to do, but we heeded the warning we were given.

Manny continued talking to him. During the conversation, El Diablo instructed one of the other guides to reorganize the groups and to line them up according to what state they were from. The lesser guide quickly did so. He called for everyone from Oaxaca, to form a line here; those from Michoacan were to form a line over there; those from Sinaloa form a third row, and so on. It was the first time I had ever witnessed polleros doing that.

Meanwhile, El Diablo kept trying to talk to me directly and was getting angry that I did not respond. "Answer me," he warned, "or I will come up there and teach you a lesson!"

Which is exactly what we wanted him to do! If we could take El Diablo down, we might get the whole mess of illegals all at once. We simply had to entice him.

"He cannot answer," Manny called down. "He is soo drunk he cannot speak."

That got El Diablo's attention. Now we just needed something to get him moving.

"We will pay to join your group," Manny continued and then informed the Devil that I was carrying the money.

It worked. That was just too irresistible for El Diablo to pass up, and here he came.

I could see that this low life had no weapon in his hands as he approached, so I carefully re-holstered my own weapon. I knew Brett had me covered and I would need both hands to bring him down, since I was already at a position of disadvantage on the ground. If I dared to stand, he would certainly realize I was Border Patrol, take off running, and sound the alarm to the others.

I was wearing a very light jacket that was partially unzipped.

The man very cautiously walked up to where I was sitting and tried to reach inside my jacket. As he bent down to search me for the money, I grabbed his head and the collar of his t-shirt and pulled him to the ground, a move he clearly wasn't expecting.

El Diablo screamed like a girl! In a panic, he jerked back so hard he pulled entirely out of his t-shirt! Right over his head it came. Once he yanked free, he ran, hollering and screaming down the road.

I suppose even the Devil could be a bit jumpy at Doghouse Junction but, after seeing the way El Diablo ran off screaming like that, I thought "El Cream Puff" would have been a more appropriate title for him.

El Diablo was heading south somewhere between light speed and Mach One. Naturally, Brett and I gave chase. Of course, by the time I got to my feet, the suspect had a good lead on me, so I ran across the hillside at an angle trying to cut him off. I came to the edge of a drop off above the road. It only looked to be a couple of feet, and I thought I could jump to the road from the embankment. Unfortunately, things are often distorted at night, and distance can be very misleading. I jumped, but I felt myself falling a lot farther than expected.

That little two-foot drop off turned out to be about ten feet. I landed hard on the rocks and fell onto the road down below. For a moment, I actually thought I had broken my legs on impact, which sucked!

By that time, total pandemonium had broken out in all the groups. El Diablo never knew we were Border Patrol because he never yelled out "Migra" to the others. He just screamed and ran, likely assuming we were bandits like he was.

Well, panic is contagious, and all 130 screaming aliens took off running in every direction. I had landed in the middle of the crowded road, but was unable to get back up. People were running by me, others were jumping over me, each one trying to get away even though none of them knew why they were running. They just saw El Cream Puff panic and followed suit.

Meanwhile, the pain in my legs was excruciating, the worst pain I had ever felt. All I could do was lie there on the ground holding my gun next to me. I kept it just out of sight, in case they figured out I was Border Patrol and took offense. Currently, they still didn't know, and that was a good thing.

I finally managed to drag myself off the road and hide in the brush like one of the aliens. In fact, there were already a couple of aliens camped out on the other side of the same set of bushes.

As it turned out, my legs were not broken, and I was eventually able to get back up. We called for more agents to come up and assist, as it was just too hard for the four of us to capture that many people at night, all at once, on the mountain, without a scope. By daybreak, however, we had caught almost 100 of the 130 or so that took flight. It was as they say, "a good lick."

We never caught El Cream Puff. He had long since reached Mexico and was last spotted halfway to Guatemala.

Sawing Logs at Doghouse Junction

Otay Mountain always provided the agents with plenty of memorable adventures and a few unexplainable ones as well. Shortly after the fire of 1996 wiped the mountain clean of vegetation, another one of the more unbelievable moments happened.

A fellow agent Pat and I were assigned to the Copper Canyon/Doghouse Junction area on a midnight shift. My partner and I were the only two agents assigned to the area that night and the mountain was ours alone. The fire-charred terrain was still blackened by a layer of black soot and, that night, a thick fog had set in as well. It was an eerie scene.

For several nights in a row, heavy fog had rolled up the canyon from south to north. It just so happened that as the fog would roll across a sensor near the bottom of Copper Canyon the bug would hit.

So, did the fog cause the sensor to activate or were groups merely walking in the fog and using it for cover from the night vision scopes? We weren't sure, but every night the fog rolled in, the sensor hit. This night was no exception. Groups would often come up out of the canyon, cross the road, and continue on toward Windmill Canyon, the KOA, or other pathways to Otay Lakes Road. This is what we assumed we were dealing with.

Pat and I parked our Broncos where the trail crossed the road. We got out of our rides and started making our way down into the canyon in an effort to intercept the traffic. It was about a thirty-five minute hike down the trail to where we thought we had the best chance at taking the group. We found our positions and laid-in to wait. And we waited. And then waited some more. But no one ever showed up. Eventually, we came to the conclusion that it must have been a false hit, which is fairly common. We had wasted a couple hours, yes, but we still got paid. No harm, no foul. Right?

By the time we hiked back up to our vehicles, it was about 3:30 a.m. We had parked our rides next to each other, but facing opposite directions. That way we could roll down the windows and talk, while still watching each other's back.

My vehicle was facing east toward the Copper Canyon, enabling me to watch the trail and see anything that came up out of the canyon. Now if you have ever worked a midnight shift for any length of time, then you know everyone takes a little nap here and there. If any agent or officer claims to have never dozed off on a midnight shift, he or she is lying. Period. The Z Monster eventually gets everyone!

Well, the Z Monster was about to get Pat. So, we worked it out that he would take about twenty minutes to relax, while I watched. Later I would count a few sheep, while he watched.

All was going according to plan, when suddenly I saw a figure walking through the fog and heading straight for us. He was on the same trail we had just laid-in on for nearly an hour. He was still out about 150 feet or so, but I could see him quite easily. I checked to see if Pat was awake yet, but he was still cutting firewood.

Then, I noticed that the individual actually looked like an agent. He was in a dark uniform and appeared to be wearing a gun belt. I inquired on the radio if there was green traffic walking up out of Copper Canyon, but got no reply. Still thinking he was one of us, I jumped out of my truck and walked toward the individual, but then wondered what another agent would be doing in Copper Canyon when only Pat and I were assigned that area. I was quite certain that no other PA could have gotten there without our knowing about it.

As we walked toward each other, I realized that it was not another agent. It now appeared that the individual was wearing a flight suit of some kind and perhaps a utility belt. I supposed it was possible there had been a plane crash earlier in the day that nobody knew about; and the pilot had survived but was just now walking up out of the canyon below. After all, there had been plenty of plane crashes in that area of the mountain.

It seemed strange.

By now, I was starting to wish that I had woken my partner up. A few seconds later, we were nearly close enough to speak. The individual did not seem to pose a threat, and even appeared to break into a bit of a smile. Then, inexplicably, his face began to glow. Without warning, he started to disappear. Right in front of me, the figure faded into a vapor-type mist and then shot past me towards the road that lay behind.

It is hard to put into words what I was thinking at that particular moment, but oddly enough, I did not feel fear. Just disbelief, I guess. It was actually kind of funny once I really thought about it.

As I mentioned, the trail I was standing on was covered in a fine powdery layer of soot and was excellent for sign cutting. Nothing could have crossed without tearing it up and leaving some very easy-to-read sign. So, I turned

*Figure 3—A view of our only road, as it parallels Copper Canyon.
Taken after the fire of 1996.*

Figure 4—A small group we caught as they tried to make it over the mountain.

Figure 5—Clouds and fog have completely engulfed Copper Canyon.
One of the antennas is visible on the peak of Otay near Doghouse Junction.

Figure 6—Small makeshift memorial made by Border Patrol Agents at the crash
site of Reba McEntire's band members.

Figure 7—A thick cloud layer in Copper Canyon. Notice you can see over and under the cloud layer.

Figure 8—Sunrise near Buttewig/Mine Canyon.
The island in the background is the peak of a 4,500 ft. mountain.

81

on my flashlight and started looking for footprints on the trail, searching for some explanation. I immediately spotted footprints: One set for me and another set for Pat, but no one else's. No other tracks were anywhere nearby—it was clean.

I went back to the road in the direction the where we had parked and cut all around there for sign as well. The mist had headed that way, but there were only my boot prints and Pat's. There were no others.

When I returned to my vehicle, I found my partner still dozing. I didn't bother to wake him. Instead, I sat in my truck and thought about what had just happened. It was then that I noticed a small tingle of fear. I had never seen a spirit or apparition before. Unfortunately, I have never seen one since, either.

Pat woke up shortly thereafter. I was busting a gut to tell somebody about what had happened, but I kept quiet and never told him. Matter of fact, I never told anyone from the station for about ten years. Even then, it was only one or two guys that I trusted, but not until right before I transferred to Kingsville, Texas, in 2007.

They would have thought I was a loon.

For Whom the Bells Toll

Shortly before I joined the Border Patrol, one of my cousins and I were having a conversation about the risk of law enforcement. She was an agent with the Oklahoma State Bureau of Investigation. I expressed my concerns to her about the level of danger and her reply was, "I don't worry about it. There are two kinds of officers who die on duty: Those who think they can never be killed, and those who know they are going to be killed."

It was a while before I gave it much thought again. I don't know if there is any truth to that statement, but many times it did seem like agents knew that something was going to happen to them.

In the summer of 1996, Border Patrol Agent Stephen Starch gave a tour to his mother while she was visiting him in San Diego. According to a newspaper article in Lubbock, Texas, his mother said she felt her worst fears wash over her as she looked out over the extremely rugged terrain and developed a very bad feeling in her gut—a mother's intuition.

She went on to say in the article, that when Stephen entered into the Border Patrol, he said that he did not think he would have a long life (*Avalanche-Journal*, 1997).

Agent Luis Santiago also expressed fears about being killed on duty and was extremely safety conscious, much more so than anyone else in our academy class or even at the station. Actually, few agents ever really expressed concern over their safety to anyone. We knew the risk when we signed on, and it was always somewhere in the back of our minds, but we never really worried about it.

On Saturday morning, June 14, 1997, Border Patrol Agent Stephen C. Starch was out on foot tracking a group of illegal aliens near Tecate Peak on Tecate Mountain. He and his partner split up to cover more ground, a common tactic. After a while, when Agent Starch's partner could no longer make contact with him on the radio, he notified a supervisor that something might be wrong and a search for him immediately began.

A request was made for air support to assist in the search, but the request was promptly denied. President Bill Clinton had come to San Diego that day, and was currently sitting on the tarmac in Air Force One preparing to leave. The President's departure had been delayed for some unknown reason; but all aircraft in the San Diego area were still grounded.

Priorities, you understand.

Another request was made to allow the launch of the Border Patrol helicopter Foxtrot, to assist in the search. It is not known if the President was made aware of the search for Agent Starch. Nevertheless, Foxtrot had requested multiple times for permission to lift off.

But again, it was denied.

The supervisors kept trying. Eventually, Foxtrot and a Coast Guard helicopter were allowed to lift off and join in the search, but too much precious time had been lost.

Approximately three hours after Agent Stephen Starch went missing, his body was found at the bottom of a cliff near Tecate Peak. He had fallen about 150 feet from the cliffs above. It was determined that he was still alive when he landed at the bottom of the cliff. He died while they were searching for him.

His death was ruled an accident.

The Bells Toll Again

Saturday, March 27, 1999, Border Patrol Agent Stephen M. Sullivan was working a midnight shift with other Brown Field agents in Buttewig Canyon on a joint operation. I reported for work that Saturday morning and attended the muster briefing like any other day, and this promised to be another uneventful, mundane Saturday morning. It was a beautiful day and the alien traffic wasn't nearly as heavy as it had previously been. Unfortunately, that's when tragedy strikes, suddenly and without warning on the dullest of days.

During the morning briefing, a supervisor mentioned somewhat casually that there might have been an accident of some sort involving an agent up on the mountain. Two illegal aliens walking the road had flagged down a passing agent and told him that a Border Patrol vehicle had just driven off the side of the mountain.

The aliens, who were inside the vehicle at the time, claimed they had been thrown out of the back as the truck went over the side. There was also a third alien thrown out who was unable to walk, but four other prisoners and the agent driving had gone over the edge of a cliff.

No one knew exactly what to make of this information as there had been no call for help over the radio, and none of our people were currently reported missing. All Brown Field agents were accounted for at the end of shift, so we were not overly alarmed. After all, aliens had made false reports before. Nevertheless, units were sent up to investigate. Once those assigned to the mountain arrived on scene, they discovered broken brush and Border Patrol truck parts lying just off the road between Buttewig and Mine Canyon, but there was no sign of the actual vehicle itself. About then, the El Cajon Station realized that one of their men was indeed missing.

El Cajon agents normally did not work this particular area, although it was a region the two stations sometimes shared. However, Agent Sullivan had been on a special operation with Brown Field agents during the night. He had just finished working a midnight shift and was last seen heading back to the El Cajon Station with seven prisoners in the back of his truck.

Brown Field agents had watched him drive away and thought nothing more of it, assuming he had made it safely back to his station. Several efforts were immediately made over the radio to make contact with the missing unit, but the calls were met with silence.

According to one of the local newspapers, one of the surviving crash victims claimed that a couple other prisoners on board were distracting Agent Sullivan as he drove the narrow mountain road, while another began taunting him.

Whether this figured into the crash or not, I don't know, but I am very familiar with that stretch of road, and know well that at dawn the sun rises up from underneath. When the sun reaches a certain elevation, the glare can suddenly and completely blind a driver. This could have easily been a factor, as investigators believe the Bronco went over the edge shortly before 7:00 a.m., around the time of sunrise.

Certainly, the two events combined would have been a deadly combination.

The road leading over the top of the mountain had recently been improved, but with a potential fatal flaw. The borders of this single lane road had been built up to widen it, but the correction had made the outer edge of the road soft. If a vehicle drove too close to the outside, the ground would give, pulling the vehicle closer to the edge.

After the improvement, a supervisor voiced his concern regarding the flaw, ominously noting that the smoother, faster road, with those soft edges, was going to get somebody killed. Those words came back to haunt us all.

On this beautiful but equally dreadful Saturday morning, I was assigned the Otay Port of Entry as my patrol area, but the only place I wanted to be was up on that mountain, looking for the missing agent. Still, everyone thought things would turn out okay. PAs went missing and lost radio contact all the time only to be found later unharmed. I was hopeful that this, too, would be one of those times.

However, as the guys on scene began to follow the truck tracks and wreckage deeper and deeper down the side of the mountain, things started looking bleak—the terrain was much steeper than it appeared from the road. At that point, the searchers had already descended several hundred feet on foot and there was still no sign of the crash site. That's when I started to get a sick feeling in the pit of my stomach.

I pulled my ride alongside that of another agent and, in silence, monitored the progress of the search over the radio. This was one of those times when none of us wanted to be alone, yet didn't feel much like talking either. We sat quietly listening to the radio and just feeling helpless, while the searchers were climbing down hand over foot. When they had reached more than a thousand feet yet still had not located the crash site, the sick feeling in the pit of my stomach grew worse.

The rescuing agents eventually reached Agent Sullivan's vehicle. Somebody just as impatient for update as the rest of us asked about his status on the radio. Border Patrol radio frequencies were not encrypted at that time, and anyone with a scanner could hear what was going on, but the rescuer, overcome by the scene, improperly announced the dreaded news over the air.

"The agent is DOA."

"Don't say that shit over the air!" an angry supervisor immediately scolded, but the news was out.

For a long time, there was only silence, as everyone listening now knew the fate of the missing agent. After a bit, the supervisor came back on the air and, in a more composed voice, asked the guys down below if there was anyone else in the vehicle that needed rescue or medical care.

The response was equally as grim. "No. They are all 10-7."

Agent Sullivan's Bronco had fallen off the cliff and tumbled over 1,200 feet to its final resting place, killing him and all four remaining prisoners—

a gruesome scene. The three aliens who survived were thrown from the back when the truck rolled over the very first time, near the top of the mountain (Protection, 1999).

They were lucky.

After Agent Sullivan's death, many PAs began driving differently on that mountain. Prior to this accident, they stayed buckled up at all times, but after Agent Sullivan's death when PAs drove along the side of any canyon with such horrendous drop offs, they took their seat belts off.

It became very clear: the only chance for survival in such horrific crashes was to be thrown from the vehicle. So, many agents, myself included, decided to take our chances on being ejected with the hope that the vehicle wouldn't roll over us because going over the edge with a fastened seat belt meant certain death.

You Be the Judge

The paranormal events discussed in this book are all legitimate sightings experienced and conveyed by reliable witnesses—events definitely qualifying as supernatural. I experienced two bizarre occurrences personally that I will share, both of which have no legitimate explanation. It is possible that both incidences were merely strange anomalies that my partner and I could not explain, but I have decided to tell the stories anyway and let you be the judge. One event is listed below, while the other event is recounted at the end of "The Little Girl in White" chapter.

Sometime around 1996, detailed agents from other areas began to arrive at the Brown Field Station to help us out a bit. They would do a thirty-day stint in San Diego and then return to their home stations.

When they initially arrived at our station, they were sent up the mountain for three consecutive nights to try it out. After three shifts on top, they were given the choice to continue working the mountain or take a different assignment sitting on X's for the remainder of their detail. After their initial three shifts, ninety-eight percent of the detailers elected not to go up the mountain again.

At the end of their thirty-day assignment, we often held a little informal barbeque for the departing detailed agents. During one of the BBQs, a detailer who had decided to work the mountain every night began to spin a yarn and recount some of his experiences.

"Man, you people have some really strange things going on up on that mountain," he said.

"How so?" asked a Brown Field agent.

The detailer explained, "The other night I was with one of your guys, and we were working a group. We had a good visual and started moving in. We could see them almost the whole way, but when we got there, they were gone!"

"Are you sure they didn't just run away?" asked the Brown Field agent.

"No sir," said the detailer. "They just vanished!"

The others laughed, but I didn't. I knew exactly what he was talking about. A couple of weeks earlier my partner Russ and I had experienced a similar event. We were walking the Otay Truck Trail one night just north of the White Cross Trail. It was a busy area, and this was an extremely dark night. So dark, in fact, that there was no chance a passing group could see us. All we had to do was stand by the road and wait for them to arrive.

Oddly enough, we waited and waited and waited some more, but nobody ever came. Sometimes on nights as dark as this, groups wouldn't move at all because they simply couldn't find their way. So Russ and I assumed that was the case and were about to call the whole thing off when we heard a single individual on the road.

From the sound of things, he was walking recklessly and carelessly and dragging his feet with each step. When you spend so much time in the dark, you become very, very good at listening. It was definitely just one person, and he was making a ridiculous amount of noise.

My partner and I were both standing on the road with Russ positioned three or four feet to the side of me. The single individual was walking right straight for us. As he got closer, each step became more distinct until, finally, the sound of his footsteps brought him directly up to me—face to face—and stopped.

Then, there was total silence.

I wondered how he knew to stop. I couldn't see him, so I knew he couldn't see me. I reached out to grab him, but there was nothing there. I stepped forward and tried again and, once more, there was nothing.

"Russ," I whispered, "where is he?"

"He's in front of you," he said.

"No he's not," I replied. "Where did he go?"

We both turned on our flashlights. There had been no footsteps leading away—we both would have heard that—but there was nobody there. Puzzled, we searched the area, but there was no one. It was very easy to cut for foot signs on the road, and we could see our own tracks quite clearly, but there was no sign for the individual who had walked up to us.

We searched a few more minutes, but eventually gave up.

Russ looked at me with an odd expression. "That was weird," he said.

"I'll say," I agreed. "Very weird. Let's get out of here."

About the same time this occurred, I recall hearing occasional reports of an individual said to be haunting that same area. We will talk more about that in much more detail in the last chapters of the book, but I wanted you to form your own opinion.

So...I'll let you be the judge.

Chapter 8
Otay Lakes and Otay Valley
Witch Weirdness

The last place we learned to work while on the training unit was the Otay Lakes area. Otay Lakes Road was the first paved road that a group of illegal aliens would encounter after crossing the Otay Mountain range and, often, their foot journey would end at that road. Once there, they would climb into a "load" vehicle driven by another smuggler and ride either toward Los Angeles, California, or stash up in one of the many local load houses in San Diego.

This was a fun area to work and was an assignment most agents preferred. Groups would come down from the KOA ridgeline from high off the mountain, pass east of the lake, and then head north to Otay Lakes Road. If the smuggler decided it was too risky to load up on Otay Lakes Road, then he would lead the group across the pavement and over the next ridgeline. The group would then continue farther north to Proctor Valley Road, where a load vehicle had a smaller risk of detection.

While on the Field Training Unit, I had worked this area twice, so I was mildly familiar with it. Eventually, the time came when I was to work the lakes alone. I remember the sun had just gone down on a swing shift when the scope operator spotted a group of thirty illegals coming down off the KOA. I answered up immediately, as I was close by, fresh off the FTU, and eager for a little action. Another agent, also nearby, came to assist.

On the west side of Otay Lake was an Olympic training center that focuses on archery and rowing, and perhaps some bicycling, but the east side of Otay Lake was a very secluded place. I had heard stories about a small group of Satan worshippers and witches in long black trench coats sometimes hanging out near the creek bottom that led into the lake. Supposedly, they would show up, build a fire, perform some weird ritual, and then sacrifice a defenseless animal.

Interesting story, but back to chasing this group.

My partner and I hid our vehicles and hiked in, trying to intercept the aliens. By following Scope's instructions, we were able to close in on the illegals without announcing our presence. We got close enough that we could hear them, but since it was an exceptionally dark that night, we still could not see them. We followed the bunch for a while before they dropped down into the creek and headed east, which is when the scope operator lost sight. There was a thick canopy over the creek, and Scope could not see through the dense vegetation. We thought we heard the group split up, as they often did when pursued, so my partner headed west and I continued east into the creek bottom.

I was still able to hear movement ahead of me and continued pursuing blindly on foot knowing I wasn't far behind. I followed the illegals deeper and deeper into the creek bottom when suddenly, I thought I heard them stop and bush up. In fact, I was sure of it.

Great, I thought. I'll just sack them all up now! Unfortunately, I still couldn't see anything. It was so dark I was tripping and stumbling over everything.

This meant turning on a flashlight to illuminate the area, thereby giving away my position, which left me in a predicament. If I was wrong and they were not bushed up, they would see my light and I would lose the whole group and every other group nearby. Then again, it was so dark that I couldn't find them anyway, so I took the chance and lit up.

Immediately upon lighting my flashlight, I saw a female body underneath the thick canopy between some large boulders. She was partially clothed. A blindfold had been wrapped around her eyes, and she was tied to a tree with her hands behind her back! My heart pounded and I jumped back, certain that I had stumbled into a murder scene.

My first thought was the ritualistic satanic sacrifices I'd heard about. Then I noticed there were animal bones scattered on the ground and tied up in the tree limbs. A couple of cooking pots and a skillet with two black feathers in it were strung about. I was in the middle of the Witch's camp.

Cold chills shot up and down my spine.

Of course, the group I was chasing had given me the slip. I saw no people hiding in the bushes or anywhere else about me. It was difficult to see through the thick brush with only a flashlight, but I shined the light on the body again and saw no movement, heard no plea for help. She was very stiff in appearance, almost plastic like, and I was certain she was dead. I assumed she had probably been there for quite a while.

This will be my first murder scene, I thought, and cautiously moved closer through the rocks and brush for a better look. When I finally reached the corpse, I got quite a surprise. The victim of this heinous crime was not a human. She was a mannequin! Yep, full size and very lifelike, but absolutely a mannequin.

At that point, I am not sure if I was relieved or even more disturbed. What kind of sicko brings a female mannequin to the bottom of a creek bed,

Figure 9–A fellow agent taking a short break as we hiked down one of the many trails leading down from the KOA. Notice plastic handcuffs sticking out of his back pocket

Figure 10—Taken in an unknown canyon, possibly Windmill Canyon. Can you find the PA?

hides it under heavy canopy and ties it to a tree with its hands behind its back, and then blindfolds it? Wow! What purpose did she serve?

Never mind. I don't want to know.

Needless to say, after that creepy little incident, I was no longer concerned about finding the group. They were long gone anyway—just thirty more people on John McCain's pathway to citizenship. This was about all I could manage for one night and left the area. I figured now was a good time to 10-3 this whole scenario and go get a cup!

Hobo Jungle Hell

In 1980, Charles Bronson starred in a movie named *Borderline*. It was filmed within the Brown Field Station's area of operations and, supposedly, is more or less a true story loosely taken from actual events. With the exception of Bronson and his co-star, all the agents in the movie were real Border Patrol agents. The illegal aliens were also real. It appears to have been filmed mainly in the Otay Valley, with the movie's final shootout taking place in Hobo Jungle.

The film crew would go out at night with an agent and wait for the other PAs to start working groups of illegals. The camera operators would then move in and start filming. Some of the agents who appeared in that movie were still at the station when I arrived in 1994.

Even though the movie had used real BP personnel and aliens, it did not capture the true essence of Hobo Jungle or the surrounding areas. It failed to expose the jungle's dark soul.

One day, I was patrolling the valley near Hobo Jungle when I ran into Jerry, the rancher that leased the area to graze his cattle. Jerry was a friendly fellow and we talked for a while.

The old cowboy gave me the low down on the valley, which I found quite interesting. He told me how one of his ranch foremen had been beaten to death by illegal aliens while opening a gate one night. A year later, his new ranch foreman was jumped at the same gate and severely beaten as well. He survived, but was in a coma for a good long while and never returned to work. Then, he told me about a group of bandits living down there for a time who had kidnapped an illegal alien husband and wife. The bandits held the couple hostage in the heavy brush near Hobo Jungle, out of sight from the passing Ram Chargers of the Border Patrol. The man they kept bound and gagged at all times and kept him alive only to use against the woman.

The woman, also bound and gagged, was raped repeatedly and in a most brutal manner. If she resisted, then things only got worse. They would wrap rope around the husband's feet and hang him upside down from one of the trees. The bandits would then stab the husband in the legs with an ice pick until the woman stopped resisting their sexual assaults. When they were through with her, they would lower the husband back down until they needed him again. This continued day and night by the gang of bandits. During this time, the husband was stabbed countless times. The ordeal lasted almost a week before the wife escaped and was rescued. I cannot remember if Jerry said whether her husband survived his ordeal, but this gives a good example of the mindset of the bandits we faced. This is what the US/Mexico border is really like. It's about drug trafficking, murder, rape, death, and carnage. This place knows pure evil. It is no wonder the spirits are so active in the Otay area.

Even as *Borderline* was being filmed, such horrors were taking place in nearby areas, though such heinous crimes were barely hinted at in the movie.

I don't think the average American can handle knowing what really happens there. When I tell these things to someone who "wants to know what it's like" or asks to hear a story, he or she will often simply look at me with a blank stare. This look relays exactly what this person is thinking: that the story is a lie made up by a racist to make illegals look bad.

My advice: If you can't handle the truth about the border, don't ask about it.

People think they know all about the border and the folk hero "Coyotes" who operate there because they ate at a Mexican restaurant once and drank a Margarita. Some of these people are our elected officials. They have preconceived notions of what the border and illegal aliens are like, and they expect me to validate what they want to be true: that the border is safe and there are just a bunch of really nice people crossing it. But it just ain't so.

Famous Last Words

Once, while I was working in the detention area of the station, things had begun to slow down a bit. Several agents were assigned processing duties, but we weren't busy and a BS session broke out instead. It feels strange to call it a BS session since there was actually far more truth in these sessions than in our daily muster briefings, but I digress.

Everyone told some funny story or unusual event that had happened and we were all having fun. Last to tell was Al, the most senior agent present. Although he was only a few of years older than I was, he had been in the Patrol about ten years longer. He was also a Vietnam Veteran and had developed quite a bizarre sense of humor about things, including death.

Years earlier Al had been on the "Bandit Team," a unit whose sole purpose was to hunt down bandits and bring them in—dead or alive. Since bandits weren't too fond of being arrested, they usually chose to shoot it out, which meant dead was often the flavor of the day.

After one of the nightly shooting competitions, all of the bandits who had been competing were currently lying on the ground, apparently dead. That night, it was Al's turn to count the bodies, and his story went something like this:

"There were four or five of them that I could see lying on the ground. They all looked dead. So, I went to each one of them, shook him, turned him over, and then would say, "This one's dead. Yep, this one's dead," and so forth. However, when I got to the last one, I didn't roll him over. I just said, "Yeah, he's dead too." The offended bandit turned himself over, looked me right in the eye, and informed me in a voice barely more than a whisper, "Not yet!" Those were the last words he ever spoke," Al said, "because he then promptly rolled himself back over and died on the spot."

To Shoot or Not To Shoot

After passing our ten-month exams, my academy classmates and I were finally cut loose from the training unit to start patrolling on our own. It was a good feeling not to be a trainee anymore. Having our every action ridiculed and analyzed had long since grown tiresome.

Alan and I were assigned to the Otay Valley for the evening, and we were ready to go. A couple hours after sundown a sensor in our area hit. It was a very reliable bug, and we knew it would be good. Now that we were off the training unit, working traffic promised to be a lot more fun!

We figured we had about fifteen minutes to get into position before the group arrived, so we walked down a little dirt road for about five minutes and found a good spot to wait. I was going to be the busting agent, and Alan would let them pass and then keep them from TBS-ing (Turning Back South and making a run back to the border). After several minutes, the group didn't come. We figured they were just slow, so, we waited some more.

While in the training unit, I had developed the habit of looking behind myself regularly, and I did so now thinking maybe these guys had given us the slip and managed to get behind us somehow. As I turned around, I noticed something on the ground directly behind me. I didn't know what it was, but it wasn't moving.

It looked like a rock.

The problem was, it had not been there before. I would have had to step over the thing to get to where I was currently standing, and I did not remember doing that! I would have remembered, too, because it was a big rock.

Now there wasn't much light out that night, but the road was lighter than the darkness that surrounded it, so it actually provided pretty good contrast for the object I was staring at. But still…what was it?

About then, I detected movement. It was slight, but looked a bit like an ear flick.

That meant it wasn't a rock.

It was an animal. A fairly large one. And brave.

I had seen a very large bobcat or possible lynx down in the valley before on previous shifts. So, after a quick calculation, I decided this one probably weighed sixty or seventy pounds. I also realized it had followed me to that spot, which meant it was probably hungry.

I considered shooting it.

At the time, I didn't know much about cats, but I did know about wounded animals. Wounded animals attack with reckless abandon; therefore, if I failed to kill the beast with one clean shot, it would go berserk on me and I would die in pieces.

I knew men back home who had hunted bear and told stories of how ferociously they would attack after being wounded, even if the shot proved later to be fatal. Then there was the account of a man who was attacked by nothing more than a small wounded bobcat, which he described as being similar to a chainsaw running at full speed.

These thoughts ran quickly through my head, so I decided it might be best to hold off on my shot for a moment and see if the cat backed off on its own. I didn't really feel like being attacked by a chainsaw.

Luck was with me that night and the cat eventually lost interest, which was good, but when it left, I noticed what I had not been able to see before.

It was huge!

The feline had been crouched tightly and lying very low to the ground. When it stood up, it stood *way* up, and sauntered off. This thing was much larger than I first thought. Then, in contrast to the lighter colored road, I could see a very thick, very long tail swinging behind it. A little bobcat, this was not. This was a full-grown mountain lion!

Arnold Schwarzekitty!

Had I shot at such close range and not instantly killed this beast, it would have definitely torn me to shreds.

Once my heart restarted, I called Alan on the radio to warn him, but by the time he turned around to look for it, the cat was already behind him. Apparently, it lost interest in him just as quickly and darted off into the night.

We unanimously decided it was best to leave the area for a while and go get a cup.

Big Game Talkers

Alan and I reported the incident when we got back to the station at the end of shift. When the other agents heard about my mountain lion, they all started talking big. The smack talking was intolerable! All of them were big game hunters, they were. Every one of them, I tell ya! Though not a single person was armed with anything more than a pistol.

Every one swore he would have killed that cat instantly. "I would never hold my fire if I had such a chance!" they vowed.

It reminded me of a Clint Eastwood movie I had seen. Clint was riding with a young cowboy who was trying to convince Eastwood of his gun fighting abilities. He would tell Eastwood's character several times over, "I'm a damn killer, I told you."

I calmly relayed a story to all those big game killers about a professional hunting guide who once told me his brother lost a leg that way. "He shot a grizzly bear," said the guide, "and the bear ate it off."

"Didn't he shoot it again?" I asked.

The guide replied, "Yes sir, he did. After the bear knocked him down and bit into his leg, he shot at it six more times with his forty-four Magnum, but he missed every shot."

"How did he miss every shot at such close range?" I asked.

"I asked my brother that same thing," said the guide, "and he said, 'I guess you just had to be there.'"

But my audience wouldn't buy it.

"Well, sooner or later," I told the others, "one of you will get your chance and we'll see what you do."

Naturally, my brave companions assured me that they would lay down a blaze of gunfire when their time arrived. Well, as luck would have it, we didn't have to wait long. No more than three or four weeks later, two agents were walking down the truck trail on the mountain one night when something came up to check them out, crossing directly in front of them. Guess what it was?

Yep. A big ol' mountain lion.

Guess how many shots these two big game hunters fired off?

Right again. None!

Best part was that one of them had been one of the smack talkers on the night of my encounter.

For those of you who think shooting dangerous big game animals at point blank range with a pistol is a good idea, here's a little food for thought.

One night, about fifteen of my fellow agents and I were going through a firearms training course at the San Diego Sector shooting range. The course was taught by a fellow agent named Jim, who had hunted big game all over the world. He had also experienced on-duty shootings in the Border Patrol and really knew his stuff. I deeply respected his opinion on such matters.

At one point during the lecture portion of the training, Jim said that all handguns were just marginal at stopping or killing suspects. "Don't expect a hardened criminal to stop his assault on you just because you shoot him," he warned. "Just remember, there is nothing more dangerous on the face of this earth than the person you just killed."

I will never forget his warning.

I think it safe to include wounded mountain lions in that as well. After several more encounters between the cats and agents, it was proving to be quite hard to kill one with nothing more than a pistol, especially without the benefit of hunting dogs, thereby prompting one of the supervisors to declare during one of our muster briefings, "Any agent who comes driving back to the station with a mountain lion draped over his fender is going to be a legend!"

Shortly after the latest cat sighting, the Bureau of Land Management folks put out a little information concerning mountain lions in our area of operations. They thought at least three to four were roaming Otay Mountain, Valley, and Lake regions, and one of them was estimated at nearly 200 pounds.

Just a couple of weeks later, an agent hiking down from the KOA found a dead body. It had all the classic signs of a cat kill and was later confirmed to be just that. The bodies of several more aliens apparently killed by mountain lions were found later throughout the rest of that year, most of them on or near the KOA ridgeline. As far as I could tell, the illegals that were killed did not go on the official California record of people killed by cats, and I do not remember reading about any accounts of their deaths in the newspaper, either.

It was actually surprising to me that many more aliens were not killed in this fashion. The lions in our area of operations had lost their natural fear of man. They had gotten a taste of human blood and, evidently, they liked it. Illegals that got left behind by their smugglers or couldn't keep up were easy meals for such an efficient predator. Anyone walking around up on the mountain alone, lost, and unarmed was pure prey. Humans had entered the food chain, and agents were no exception.

Agents were continually stalked, sized-up, but then typically left unharmed. Rarely was the agent even aware he had been followed. If a lion doesn't want you to know he's there, you won't. You will not hear or see him unless he wants you to.

It was amazing to me that no PA was ever attacked during any of these feline encounters, with the exception of Agent Dalton Conner, who did the attacking. The only explanation I can think of is that the cats recognized the PAs as fellow predators. After all, we moved deliberately and acted differently from the groups we were seeking, which was our prey. We put off a different vibration, I guess.

There is really no way to know.

Once, after running down a group on foot in the valley, I started walking back to my ride. I was backtracking the group's sign with a flashlight to see if I had missed anyone. I could see my own tracks on top of the groups' tracks, but on top of mine was another set—that of a cat. While I was running behind the group of aliens, a cat had been running behind me! Whether it was a small lion or just a large bobcat, I couldn't tell, but it left me feeling quite uneasy.

102

Unrest at the Indian Diggs

The week I retired from the patrol, I was talking to Agent Munguia, a friend and classmate of mine from the Border Patrol Academy. We were both sent to Brown Field Station to start our careers. Actually, our entire academy class had been sent to the Brown Field Station. It was the first time that an entire class was sent to the same station.

Anyway, I had heard of a paranormal event that Agent Munguia was involved in very early in our careers and wondered if it was true. I had heard about the event several times throughout the years, but had never asked him directly about it. During our conversation, he retold the story to me and assured me that it was indeed true. What he relayed to me matched exactly with what others had said.

I asked Agent Munguia if he minded my using his story in my book about paranormal experiences within our Border Patrol work environment. He didn't mind and graciously gave me permission to retell his experience. He felt as I do on such matters, that if a story is true and actually happened, then it should be told without fear or worry of what others might think. If others don't like it, then that's too bad. After all, they weren't there. Nor would most of them ever dare go there, either.

The Indian Diggs were a section of Otay Valley, partially fenced off, where archaeologists were excavating Indian relics such as arrowheads and pottery. However, the site seemed to be cold at the time because I hardly ever saw anyone that appeared to be an archaeologist working in the area.

Agent Munguia was working his shift in Otay Valley one night when he decided to sit blacked-out near the Indian Diggs. Sitting blacked-out meant every light on the outside and inside of the vehicle was completely turned off or blackened by any means possible. Black electrical tape was the most common item found inside a Border Patrol unit. It would be used to tape over all the inside lights that could not be otherwise turned off. Sitting blacked out enabled the agent to see outside of his vehicle into the surrounding area.

It was a fairly slow night, and Agent Munguia was taking advantage of

103

it by kicking back and relaxing in his unit for a couple of hours. It was a busy time and had been a hard week. Agents learn to take a break whenever they can, because they have no control over what time business will come. After about an hour or so, his break time was suddenly interrupted.

A few yards outside of his unit, Agent Munguia could see a figure approaching directly in front of the windshield. He sat up straighter to get a better look and couldn't believe his eyes. Coming right at him was what appeared to be a Native American Indian warrior in historical dress.

"He was in a half crouched position as if sneaking up on me for an attack," said Munguia. "He had something drawn back in his hand that looked like a tomahawk or hatchet, but it didn't have a blade. I'm not sure what it was, exactly, but it scared the crap out of me. I jumped out of the truck and drew my gun, but he ran off to the other side of the vehicle. I was looking all around for him, but couldn't find him anymore. I turned on my flashlight and looked around some more, but he was gone. I started cutting the area for sign, but couldn't find any. It was the weirdest thing I've ever experienced."

Now, I know what you're thinking—a tired agent working alone at night in a remote area. He was sleeping, he was dreaming, or just had an overactive imagination.

I don't think so.

Although agents may occasionally doze off for a moment, I have never heard of one getting a dream confused with reality. As a matter of fact, people who work during the night a lot—law enforcement and soldiers primarily—learn to doze in a way that the general population is unfamiliar with and probably cannot understand. So, I will use this opportunity to explain something about our world.

Most agents and law enforcement officers are capable of lightly sleeping and even running a dream, all while still monitoring the radio. If our star number was called, we snapped out of it and came to immediately. A person is able to sleep to the point of dreaming, but is still capable of consciously monitoring his or her surroundings. In this state, a person can operate on two separate levels of consciousness simultaneously, without the two overlapping each other. The agent does not get these confused. Some people think this is not possible, but those in the business who can do it know exactly what I am talking about.

But remember, Agent Munguia said he was only relaxing and still very much awake, not sleeping. When a similar event happened to me up on the mountain, someone outside of law enforcement suggested maybe I, too, was sleeping. I was not. I was fully awake and know what I saw.

Since I know Agent Munguia personally, I can vouch for his character. He is a big guy. Prior to law enforcement, he had considerable boxing experience. This was not the kind of man to spook easily. If I could only take one guy into a fight with me, I'd pick him. It would be a no brainer.

Curious, I checked out the description of the weapon he said the Indian warrior was carrying. Agent Munguia was not from San Diego, nor was he familiar with the local Indian tribes. I thought it strange that he described the weapon as being something other than a tomahawk, but that looked a little bit like one. The tribes I knew of all carried tomahawks, but I wasn't from San Diego, either. So, I did some research on the predominant local tribe, the Kumeyaay, and found out some pretty interesting things. The first thing I was able to find out was that the Kumeyaay apparently did not use tomahawks. Instead, they used what they called a war club. It had a stick for a handle somewhat like a traditional tomahawk, but instead of a blade or sharpened stone for the head, there was a block of rounded wood.

Agent Munguia also said the apparition of the Indian warrior had on some kind of headdress, which did not look like the traditional headdress made solely of feathers sticking up, like the Cherokee or Sioux, etc.

When I looked up pictures of Kumeyaay warriors, it was easy to see that their headdresses were far different from the headdresses I had seen on other tribes. Having grown up in Oklahoma, I am quite familiar with different Native American attire and weapons, but the Kumeyaay weapons and dress did not look like anything that I had seen before. However, they did resemble the warrior Agent Munguia had described.

105

So, do I believe his story? I most certainly do. If I didn't, I wouldn't share it with you.

Actually, the stories of paranormal activity that I have heard throughout my career have rarely come from agents who are easily spooked or scared. I also did not include tales from the guys and gals that were known to be windy, exaggerate, or just plain lie. Liars were rare anyway. If a Border Patrol employee was ever caught lying on a memo, he or she was fired.

The majority of the accounts in this book come from some of the best agents that have ever served in the U.S. Border Patrol. Agents encounter these events because they are not afraid to go into the mountains and canyons in the dead dark of night. They go where some might say "angels fear to tread," and they often go there alone. These individuals are the ones that brought back the stories of bizarre, hair-raising events, not the ones who stayed behind and volunteered for processing or desk duties every night.

Unfortunately, those who willingly stay behind are often the first ones to ridicule and express doubt about another agent's field experience. Mighty brave for someone who wasn't there, I'd say.

Chapter 9
Marron Valley
Cold Reality

The morning of February 9th, 1998, started off like every other day that month: cold and wet. The Border Patrol put out numerous announcements and countless warnings telling people not to cross the mountains during the winter months; many had already died doing so. Yet the aliens continued to pour in, choosing to believe their smugglers instead. Articles filled the newspaper about the lost, the freezing, the dying, and the dead. Still, the people didn't listen. The coyotes and polleros were their folk heroes. Where the polleros led the pollos followed. Unfortunately, the reward for this blind trust often led to death, not a trip to the promised land.

One day at the beginning of my shift, I was driving leisurely down Marron Valley Road drinking my coffee and enjoying the crisp morning air. All was quiet. As I neared the intersection of Marron Valley Road and the

Otay Truck Trail, an agent put out a call for assistance. I was very near the area, so I responded. Elbert, a friend of mine, was also close by and responded as well.

I arrived on scene to find a very wet, very cold young woman excitedly trying to explain to the PA already there that her mother and grandmother needed help. Her grandmother had collapsed and could not walk. "She might be dying!" exclaimed the young woman.

The PA who called for help spoke very little Spanish and could not understand what she was saying. Many illegals speak very poor Spanish, so if the agent's Spanish skills are also lacking, it leads to very limited communication.

Shortly thereafter, Elbert, an excellent linguist, arrived and started talking with the young woman. He quickly determined that the mother and grandmother were down a trail, just off the road about a half a mile away. He told her to show us, and the young woman led us to where her mother and grandmother were.

At first, while we were standing on the road above them looking down into the ravine, we thought it might not be too hard to get them out, even though we still did not know exactly what was wrong with the old woman. The sides of the ravine were only thirty or forty feet deep, it appeared, and were steep, but we could manage.

As we started our way down toward the distressed women, we realized that not only was the little canyon very, very steep, but it was also quite muddy. We slipped and fell pretty much the whole way down.

When we reached the women, the grandmother was completely unresponsive, but alive. Her eyes were open and her pupils had constricted so small they were barely visible. She could not stand or speak. The woman who was with her was wet and shaking uncontrollably. We tried to speak with her to find out what was wrong, but she made no sense either.

The grandmother who was also soaking wet was not shivering, and we decided it must be hypothermia. It did not feel that cold to us, but the women had been out all night.

The granddaughter eventually relayed to us they had fallen in the Tijuana River the night before and had no change of clothing. Then we knew the old woman was simply freezing to death and didn't appear to have much time left. Insects, particularly ants, were already crawling all over her near lifeless body and in her hair, but the poor woman wasn't even capable of brushing them off.

Elbert and I tried to form a chair or hammock using our arms like we had been taught in first aid/rescue class and carry the old woman that way. It was difficult at best. We tried getting back up the way we had come down, but it was too steep and too muddy. We fell several times, dropping the helpless woman each time.

It was only 100 feet back to our vehicles. They were so close—if we could just get her up the hillside. Otherwise, we would have to carry her out along the bottom, which would be about a half-mile hike. We didn't believe the grandmother had that much time. We had long since called for an ambulance, but it was doubtful one would be able to get to where we were. Therefore, when we finally managed to get her out, we would need to take her to wherever the ambulance would be waiting.

Elbert and I tried several more times to get her up the hill, but it just couldn't be done and we were left with no choice but to carry her out the long way through the canyon bottom.

My partner and I tried again to carry her as a team, but it wasn't working. Every few steps one of us would fall and take the other two down. It became obvious the only way to carry the woman was for one of us at a time to just put her over our shoulder and carry her draped down our backs like a sack of feed—the fireman's carry. We had tried to carry her in a more dignified manner up to this point, but the terrain and mud just wouldn't permit it. If we were to save this woman's life, we would have to forgo niceties and do it any way we could.

So, we tried it.

We had already spent valuable energy initially trying to get her up the short side of the hill, so we were already fatigued by the onset of Plan B. The bottom of the ravine was muddy, full of brush, and unstable. But finally we managed to get her to a little firebreak, an eight-foot clearing to help slow wildfires. After a short while, however, Elbert and I were exhausted.

About that time, another agent showed up to help, and what a welcome sight he was! He had a fresh pair of legs and was bigger than both of us. The agent took the woman, hoisted her over his shoulder like a sack of potatoes, and took off with her. It looked crude, but she was out of time.

A 4 x 4 was waiting by the time the woman was finally lifted out of the canyon. We loaded up the grandmother, mother, and daughter into it and sent all three generations to the ambulance, which was idling about five miles away.

Upon arriving, the paramedics immediately went to work on the ladies, removing their wet clothes, taking temperatures and vitals. An agent followed the trio to the hospital and informed us of their condition later that day.

When I spoke to him later, he told me the old woman's body core temperature had reached as low as eighty-seven degrees. The hospital staff said they had never seen anyone still alive with a core temperature that low, but the old woman survived and was soon reunited with her daughter and granddaughter.

The attending agent spoke with the women at the hospital and inquired as to how they wound up alone on the mountain. The women said, originally, they were a part of a group of thirty—twenty-seven men and three women. The women had fallen into the river the night before and were all freezing. Because they were so cold, they had a hard time keeping up with the men, so the group left them behind to die. When we found the women, they had no food, no water, and no backpacks containing dry clothes, even though they had started their journey with all those things.

So the mother, daughter, and grandmother had started their passage with a foot guide and twenty-six other men for protection, but once things got a little rough, the coyote and all twenty-six of those brave men abandoned them.

Unfortunately, the truth was even uglier than that.

Later that day, we caught twenty-seven men a few miles north of where we found the women. We asked them if there had been women in their group and they admitted there had been. All the men had food, water, and backpacks with dry clothing. Any of them could have given the ladies dry clothes to change into, but they didn't. Not only did they not share their supplies, but had actually stolen the women's backpacks and supplies to use for themselves.

Many of the men in the group were from the same small village as the women and even claimed to be their friends, though they had done nothing to help them. When we asked why they had left girls behind to die, we were met with a barrage of excuses.

"We were really worried about them," they lied. "We didn't want to leave them behind, but they couldn't keep up and we wanted to get through. We hoped you would find them somehow."

It made me sick to listen to these dirtbags.

All the agents present wanted to give them the beating they so richly deserved, but the law protected their rights, even though the women's rights, as far as the men were concerned, were entirely meaningless. I told them I wished the very same thing would happen to every one of them on their next crossing, and I hoped that nobody found them.

These are the kinds of men who are the first to get in line when our pathetic politicians give out amnesty.

Is that the meaning of "comprehensive immigration reform"?

The Most Disturbing Words Ever Spoken

One afternoon, I was driving east on Highway 94 just east of Marron Valley Road when one of the mountain sensors hit. I was the closest agent to the area, and went to check it out. When I got near, I stashed my ride and walked into the draw where I expected the traffic to come from. Once I got into the area, I noticed a person hiding under a bush. Without a doubt, the man was an illegal alien. It was obvious he had just hiked over the mountain, because his clothes were filthy and he had sticks matted in his hair. However, as I walked up to the suspect, I noticed he had a very crazy look in his eyes—this guy was definitely was not all there. Once I began to talk to him, it became even more obvious how crazy he was.

One thing that had been driven home to all agents throughout the Border Patrol Academy was never to take custody of a drunk or crazy person, because illegal alienage cannot be reliably established. So, even though I knew this person was undoubtedly an illegal alien, there was nothing I could do except walk away.

As I turned to do so, the suspect spoke.

"Officer, you can arrest me if you want to," he said.

I turned back to him and asked, "Why would I want to do that?"

The suspect's voice became very clear and his eyes grew very intense. "Because, I like to hurt little kids," he said.

That reply sent chills through me. I immediately went back and handcuffed the suspect without further conversation.

Once I arrived at the station with the suspect, the Supervisor and FOS were quite upset with me. They reminded me that Border Patrol agents are never to arrest mentally disturbed people under any circumstance. I relayed what the suspect had told me about liking to hurt little kids and their reply was, "That is no excuse."

I was quite angry that policy was clearly more important than children's lives, so I went ahead and fingerprinted the suspect. Sure enough, his record reflected his words. This dirtbag had done several years in state prison for the torture and death of a child under four years old.

You may wonder why this man was released from prison. It's because there is a well-meaning but stupid idea shared by judges, lawyers, and citizens alike. It goes like this: "We don't want to pay for this prisoner, so let's just send him back to Mexico, and we will never see him again!"

This line of thinking is foolish and dangerous and is a mental disorder in itself. On average, convicts usually cross back into the United States illegally within seventy-two hours of their release.

Once an alien starts crossing illegally, he or she never stops. Ever.

Trainee Fright Night

After about three years, I was considered to be fairly salty. The supervisors sometimes gave me little assignments on the side, such as sending me to retrieve some NUG to prevent him from doing something stupid. For instance, some PA with about a year in service might think it a good idea to hike to the bottom of Copper Canyon on the midnight shift—oh, say…in the fog. It was common for the NUG and his or her partner to get turned around in said fog and become hopelessly lost, thereby requiring rescue and causing the supervisor on duty plenty of unnecessary headaches.

To prevent this, I might be sent out to make contact with said NUG and make sure he stayed on top of the Otay Truck Trail. Air support does not go up the mountain in bad weather or fog. Sometimes, just being dark was reason enough for the helicopter to stay off the mountain. After all, Otay Mountain had claimed its share of aircraft. Copper Canyon was more than 3,500 feet from bottom to top, so searching for lost agents in Copper at night without air support was no small task.

Yet, despite the supervisor's best efforts, this very scenario played out all the time. One night, while the mountain was covered in heavy fog, all available agents were sent up to look for a couple of NUGs. The entire patrol group did a double shift looking for them. To say the shift commander was not pleased that night was an understatement.

One midnight shift, I was given just such an assignment. Some young new Field Training Officers had just received their new class of trainees and planned to take the trainees to do a lay-in in Marron Valley until daybreak.

One of the supervisors was a little concerned about such a plan and privately pulled me aside. Just in case, he instructed me to go hang out a little north of their location and just monitor them on the radio. "Don't let them know you're there," he said, "and don't interfere, unless they get into trouble and call for help."

So, I quietly hovered a mile or two north of the training unit. All night I sat there just waiting and listening to their radio traffic. Everything went well and was uneventful until about five o'clock in the morning. It was still dark, but close to daybreak. All the trainees and their Field Training Officers were out on foot, laying in on trails and hoping to catch a few aliens.

One of the trainees radioed to his FTO that he could hear some woman screaming for her lost child and thought the woman was maybe a hundred yards or so away. The FTO instructed the trainee and his partner to make their way down and find out what was going on.

A minute or so later I heard the trainee radio back that they were nearly to the woman's location. A couple of seconds later, that same trainee called over the radio again, this time rather alarmed. "She doesn't have a face!" he relayed.

It actually sounded like he made the comment without knowing his radio mic was live. It was "an excited utterance." I figured the trainee probably had his thumb on the mic button and inadvertently clinched it when the sight of the faceless woman caught him by surprise.

Then there was silence.

After a few seconds, one of the Training Officer's radioed the trainee. "Is everything okay?"

The trainee replied, "Yeah, I think so."

The FTO radioed back, "Just stand by. I'll be right there."

There were no more radio communications concerning the matter, so I did not feel the need to go down and stick my nose in their business. Had there actually been a person, deceased or living, without a face, there would have been a firestorm of additional calls for help.

Besides, I already knew what the trainees had just witnessed. It was the second time I had heard of an agent encountering a person in Marron Valley without a face. About a year earlier, I had heard a similar story from Lupe, one of my supervisors. One of Lupe's buddies was a supervisor at the El Cajon station. A Marron Valley sensor had banged off one night and the El Cajon supervisor went down to work the bug. He found a bush to hide behind and waited for the traffic to come down the trail. A few moments later, his wait was over.

A single figure came walking down the pathway. He did not say if it was male or female, but he let the person pass, as we often do. Sometimes the rest of the group is following shortly behind, a guy doesn't want to play his cards too early. When no one else came along, though, the supervisor turned to follow the walker. The figure stopped and turned around toward the agent, but the individual had no face! Where the face should have been, there was nothing but a dark mass. Immediately afterward, the figure simply disappeared.

As for the screaming woman, the child she was looking for was a little girl in a white nightgown. The apparition of the little girl had been witnessed on numerous occasions roaming the mountain between Mine Canyon and Marron Valley at night alone. Everyone who had seen the child thought she was about three years old. Of all the reported sightings of apparitions seen at the Brown Field Station, it was this little girl that traumatized and disturbed agents the most. She will be discussed in the next chapter.

Turn Me Loose!

Marron Valley Road runs north and south, while the Otay Truck Trail runs east and west. Chicken Ranch Road is a shortcut road that runs at a forty-five degree angle connecting the two roads together. The north end of Mine Canyon, the Otay Truck Trail, and Chicken Ranch Road all converge at the same intersection.

Chicken Ranch Road is little more than a two-track road crossing open fields, but it can save several miles and minutes when used as a shortcut. It is, however, closed to the public.

Chicken Ranch Road is the setting for a story so unlikely that, had there not been so many witnesses at the scene, I would not believe it myself. I did not know Dalton Conner at the time of its occurrence, but later we worked the same shift and became friends.

Dalton was one of those agents that things just happened to. Things that would happen to no one else would find their way to Dalton. Although he sported an Anglo name, he was actually Chilean. He acquired citizenship through his father, served in the United States Army, and then joined the Border Patrol. He was a colorful character and quite a smooth talker, a very talented artist as well.

One night while Dalton was a trainee at the Brown Field Station, he was riding with his training officer around Chicken Ranch Road. At that time, Brown Field and the El Cajon Station had overlapping areas of responsibility. Chicken Ranch Road and Marron Valley was one of those areas.

An El Cajon scope operator had spotted a group of about thirty or more illegals near Chicken Ranch Road. Dalton and his training officer were the closest units to the area, so they took the call.

The scope operator noticed what appeared to be the foot guide crawling into a bush some fifty to seventy yards of ahead of the group. This was actually quite normal as the guide would come up a trail and check things out, then go back and retrieve the group. So Scope instructed the training officer to go for the group, and told Dalton to go for the guide hiding in the brush. Then the scope operator got a little weird. In a bizarre twist, he instructed Dalton to jump on top of the guide and put his hand over the man's mouth to keep him quiet.

Being a trainee and wanting to make a good impression, Dalton Conner did exactly as he was told. He snuck up to the bush, dove right on top of the unsuspecting guide, and grabbed at him with both hands. All went exactly as planned…except for one small thing.

It wasn't a foot guide. It was a mountain lion.

The "foot guide" that the scope operator had seen bushing up was actually a wild cat that had been stalking the group of aliens!

Well, the cat went ballistic, ape $#!%, and bananas—all at the same time.

How is it, you may wonder, that an agent could sneak up on a mountain lion? Well, the wind was blowing from south to north, so the cat only smelled the group. It never caught Dalton's scent, as he was coming from the north. It had focused so intently on the illegals that it failed to hear Dalton come up behind it. And Dalton, an ex-soldier with extensive jungle warfare training in Panama, knew how to get around quietly in the brush.

Of course, the cat was taken totally by surprise.

When Dalton landed on him, the animal came unwound like a tightly coiled spring. It screamed and fought to get out of Dalton's grasp. Dalton screamed and tried to let go. The furious cat took a swipe at Dalton's throat and would have gotten him, too, but its claws got hung up on his ballistic vest. The strike came within an inch of killing Dalton on the spot and his shirt was ripped to shreds.

Then, the horrified lion took off, running straight for Dalton's training officer farther down the trail.

The training officer tried to draw his firearm, but was so badly shaken he lost his grip and dropped it on the ground. You don't know what fear is until you've heard an oncoming mountain lion scream at you from twenty feet away. It is like nothing you've ever heard before.

A Border Patrol helicopter that had been hovering nearby to help work the group flew over and illuminated the area with its powerful searchlights. The pilot did manage to see the cat as it ran away from the scene, but nobody was going to stop it from escaping.

Dalton was taken to the hospital as a precaution, probably to restart his heart, but everything checked out fine.

"Another inch and you'd be dead," said the emergency room doctor. "You're very lucky."

But, Dalton knew that already. We all did. Other than a torn shirt, the man didn't have a scratch on him.

I've always told trainees that were assigned to me, "Once or twice in your career, no matter how good you are, nothing will save you but luck." I cannot tell you how many times I have seen that play out.

As for the scope operator, I guarantee this guy walked with a limp after the explosive butt chewing he received. This was a rare instance where instead of saving an agent from harm, Scope almost got him killed.

Dalton was the only agent in our station who'd ever attacked a mountain lion and lived to laugh about it. He continued to wear that shredded shirt occasionally as a badge of honor. It was an honor he had certainly earned, and nobody ever told him to change it.

Bee Canyon

Just a thousand feet or so to the east of Marron Valley sits a place called Bee Canyon. Knowing the way Border Patrol agents name places, it is entirely believable that, once upon a time, someone spotted a bee flying around down there. Hence the name.

Bee Canyon is a piece of real estate that has changed hands within the Patrol more times than a bottle of vodka in a Soviet tank crew. It eventually ended up in the hands of Brown Field during the time I served there; however, at the time of the following event, it was part of the Campo Border Patrol Station's area of responsibility.

This incident involves two agents that I do not know personally, but the story comes to me by way of a retired third party PA with an impeccable reputation.

The now retired Agent Spaulding was the Resident Agent in Charge and Agent Opel was a supervisor at the Campo Station, though I am unsure whether these were their positions at the time of the occurrence.

The two agents were working traffic together in Bee Canyon during the middle of winter one night and had laid in on opposite sides of the trail coming out of the canyon.

Suddenly, a young looking Mexican appeared and called out to the agents. "Oficial, prende la luz." (Officer, turn on the light.)

Agent Spaulding and Agent Opel both immediately turned on their flashlights and *poof*...the young man was gone. To the agents' great surprise, the apparition had simply disappeared.

Throughout this book, the reader will notice that a few of the ghosts or apparitions are residual in nature, like a playback of past events. The overwhelming majority of the supernatural encounters mentioned herein are known as intelligent hauntings, meaning the apparitions purposely approach and interact with the person they are presenting themselves to, often speaking with them directly. By far, these are the most disturbing types of encounters. The Bogeyman of Otay Mountain comes in many different varieties.

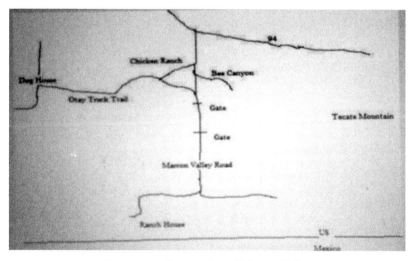

Figure 11—Basic outlay of Marron Valley.

Chapter 10
The Little Girl in White
Whose Child is This?

Charley had been around for a while. He was "Old Patrol," as we would say. The old agent spoke his mind and didn't care what anyone thought about it, but even old timers keep some things to themselves until they are ready to relinquish the tools of their trade. Charley and I had a good working relationship for the nearly ten years we served together, but the time of his retirement was near and, one afternoon while killing time in his office, he shared this story with me.

A couple of years earlier, Charley and his partner were parked where Chicken Ranch Road and the Otay Truck Trail meet. No one lives anywhere near the area and the road is lightly traveled. At the intersection, there is a fairly large tree right at the corner of the two roads.

Around three o'clock in the morning, Charlie and his partner both developed a weird feeling, like something was wrong, and began looking around. Right away, their attention was drawn to the big tree at the intersection. There, standing underneath the tree, was a very young girl about three years old in a little white gown. She was beside the trunk with her eyes fixed on them, and she was alone.

Charlie noticed a faint glow to her. He and his partner both knew the child was not alive, especially dressed like she was and all alone in such a remote place. She was clearly an apparition. Both agents just stared at the child for a moment, frozen and unable to speak, and unsure what to do next.

A few seconds later, the girl faded away, leaving Charlie and his partner with strong, lingering feelings of sadness and anxiety. They never knew why she appeared, but both were certain that in the past the little girl must have lived somewhere nearby and that something very bad had happened to her.

Mine Canyon Sighting

Charley was not the only agent that claimed to have encountered that particular young ghost. Years earlier, another agent told me of the night he encountered a little girl in white.

Agent Thomas was working the midnight shift on the east side of the mountain. He was riding alone as was normal, but there was another agent in the general area. Around 3:00 a.m., a sensor had banged off somewhere in the Mine Canyon. Agent Thomas responded. His partner responded as well, but radioed in it would be several more minutes before he could get there. Agent Thomas decided not to wait and started hiking solo up the ridgeline in Mine Canyon.

Once Thomas was in place, he began his normal routine: watch, wait, and listen. Several minutes went by with nothing amiss, but then he noticed a figure wearing white walking along the ridgeline.

"What an idiot!" he thought. "Who tries to sneak around at night dressed in white?"

122

He decided it was probably some guy wearing his lucky t-shirt who just didn't have the good sense to cover it in the dark.

Thomas watched for a while before realizing he was not looking at some dude in a t-shirt; he was looking at someone much smaller—a little girl, in fact. The agent thought she was wearing a nightgown, but said it could have been a dress—he was not exactly sure which. The girl seemed to have a very slight glow about her, which he thought was strange, he relayed later, but he assumed it was because she was dressed in white and reflecting moonlight. He wondered how in the world she had gotten on top of a ridgeline in Mine Canyon to begin with, and then realized she was walking on the ridgeline by herself!

There was a good distance between Agent Thomas and the small child, but he could plainly see there was no one with her. He worried that she had been left behind or had become separated from a group. There were no homes, campers, or tourist areas anywhere nearby, so he doubted she was a local. So, how had a child her age made it so far over such treacherous terrain with a group of illegals? He couldn't imagine. One thing was for sure, though: she would never survive on her own. Any child walking alone on the mountain was as good as dead.

Agent Thomas left his position and quickly headed for the child. As he got closer, a sense of urgency swept over him and, before he knew it, he was running. Just before he reached the child, however, she vanished.

Agent Thomas was stunned. She had been a ghost. When he realized he'd seen the mere apparition of a small child, he became very distressed over the matter and eventually fell into a depression.

"It brought tears to my eyes thinking about that little girl," he recounted later. "She was barely more than a baby."

Guardians of the Gate

There is a very small creek running along a portion of the valley bottom that parallels Marron Valley Road. Sometimes it has water, other times it doesn't.

On this road, there were two heavy iron gates about a mile apart, locked to keep the general public out of the south end of Marron Valley. It was always said that the first gate was haunted, and many agents didn't like getting out at night to open it. The south end of Marron Valley was BLM property and Border Patrol agents were some of the few who were allowed access.

While working in the processing area, one of the female Field Operations Supervisors, FOS Milano, told a couple of us that she absolutely believed the gate in question was haunted and avoided going there. "It feels like somebody is always there watching," she said. "I can feel cold spots pass through me when I'm there."

As crazy as that sounded, I had heard others say the same thing.

Field Operations Supervisor Salinetti, who was present at the time of the previous conversation with Milano, echoed that opinion. FOS Salinetti went on to say, "One night, I was working on the Otay Truck Trail when an apparition walked right by me, very near that same gate."

Mind you, these are very courageous statements from people with authority and each with so much to lose by publicly opening themselves up to unnecessary ridicule.

I absolutely believed them.

After hearing this, I learned of another incident.

One of the scope operators had been assigned to set up the night vision scope in Marron Valley. As he was driving south on Marron Valley Road, he stopped to unlock the first gate. Completely unaware of such stories, he got out of his truck and walked toward the heavy metal gate. However, before he could unlock the apparatus, he encountered the little girl in white, but this time, she was faceless. The agent was scared out of his wits! In sheer terror, he ran back to his truck.

While hastily trying to escape the area, he wrecked the truck and did considerable damage to the night vision scope. Three days later, that agent resigned his position and left the Border Patrol. Keeping his job simply wasn't worth the risk of encountering the little girl again.

Well, I cannot entirely say I blame him. I knew those gates well and often felt the same discomfort. A couple of years passed, though, before I heard more of this unfortunate child. Then one day I was sent to Marron Valley, which was common enough. It was somewhat unsafe to be in the south end of Marron Valley alone, however, so another agent and friend Sal was appointed to the area as well. Though both were assigned to the region, we had ridden in separate vehicles. As evening came about and our shift came to an end, we started heading back to the station. Sal left a few moments ahead of me.

As I was leaving the south end of Marron Valley Road, I saw an El Cajon unit passing through as he headed toward Tecate Peak, but I did not speak with him as he was too far away. I thought nothing of it. El Cajon agents often used Marron Valley to access part of Tecate Mountain, which was their area at the time.

A couple miles down the road, however, I passed through the gates and caught back up with Sal, who was parked on the side of the road. He had a rather serious look on his face and said there was something he wanted to tell me.

Apparently, he had just encountered the same El Cajon unit near the first gate and said the agent was really shaken up. The El Cajon agent told Sal that he had just gotten out of his vehicle and walked over to open the gate when he looked over at the creek next to the road. In it, he noticed a little girl floating face down in the water. She was wearing a white nightgown.

The agent raced back to his truck and, leaning half in and half out of the vehicle, grabbed the radio mic to call for help. As he was about to make the call, he looked back at the creek, but the little girl was no longer there. This time, she was standing by his vehicle, right next to him, looking up directly at him!

The agent froze.

A few seconds later, she was gone.

When Sal told me this, we were still very near the scene and chills ran over my skin. As I mentioned, many agents have reported seeing apparitions throughout the years. Usually, it had no great effect on them as a result of the sighting; it was merely chalked up as an interesting and sometimes a funny experience; however, in every case involving the little girl in white, the agent or agents involved admitted that they were emotionally distraught afterwards.

An Attorney's Artwork

A couple of years later, I had the misfortune of being in need of legal counsel. I had made an appointment with a fairly upscale law firm in one of the downtown San Diego high-rises and took the elevator up to the floor where the office was located. The door opened up inside the attorney's office, right at the receptionist's desk, and a very elegant older lady greeted me. She was extremely pleasant and showed me to the waiting area.

The office decor was quite impressive as well and, as I sat down, I could not help but notice a very striking work of art near my seat. It was a large oil painting of a very pretty young girl. Behind her was a secluded wooded area with a very dark background, obviously nighttime. The girl in the painting was wearing a white dress, and there was large tree directly behind her.

As I sat surveying the painting, I noticed the girl's lower body grew misty below the knee. She blurred, and then the image disappeared entirely. The girl in that beautiful work of art had been merely an apparition.

I was startled and immediately inquired about the painting. "Is there a story behind this piece?" I asked the receptionist. "Is it local?"

The woman said she thought the artist was local, but knew nothing else about the painting. "It's just always been here," she shrugged.

I wondered if this could somehow be related to the ghost girl in Marron Valley. It probably wasn't, but I could not help making that connection anyway. It made me wonder who was this little girl, and what was her story?

Nobody knows.

In the early eighteen hundreds, certain select people in the area had been given large land grants. A few decades later, silver was mined on Otay Mountain, and a few settlers had lived there in the early 1900s to work the mines. In fact, the canyon immediately west of Marron Valley is named Mine Canyon for that very reason. I once found an old Model T Ford in one of the draws in that area, so I am guessing the miners were there during that period. However, I have no idea when the mines were originally opened, nor do I know when they were closed or when the area was abandoned. Occasionally, people find part of a rock wall and/or foundation of what previously was somebody's home, so it was once a bustling area.

It was common knowledge also that, over the years, many people living in Marron Valley were robbed and murdered, along with several women who were raped by Mexican bandits right inside their very homes. Mexican soldiers had frequently gotten in on the act, too, crossing the border illegally to commit similar crimes on American soil.

In one incident during the 1970s or 1980s, Border Patrol agents actually ambushed a squad of Mexican soldiers that had just robbed a house on the U.S. side of the border. Even though the Border Patrol agents were outnumbered, they were in a position of advantage and got the drop on the soldiers. The soldiers decided not to resist and laid down their arms, so the agents took them into custody and transported them back to the station for processing. At least, that is what I heard from an Old Timer.

A couple of miles below the second and southernmost gate in Marron Valley, there is an old abandoned ranch house. The house sits only a few feet north of the Mexican border. The last ranch foreman who lived there, before the place was abandoned completely, and possibly his family was murdered by Mexican smugglers and stuffed down into the water well. Maybe this is where the little phantom girl once lived before meeting her tragic end. Could the faceless woman often seen in the valley calling for her child be the girl's mother?

I searched the Internet for history or some clue concerning this child or any other tragedy in Marron Valley, but was unable to come to any conclusion. I have no idea who this child may be. All the information I found was circumstantial at best, and there have been many tragedies in the area over the last one hundred eighty years. I was quite disappointed that I could not determine her identity, and it seems her story has been lost in time.

While trying to track down information on this particular ranch foreman's murder, I discovered information about other murders committed by Mexican bandits and Indian attacks dating all the way back to 1837. In one of the 1837 murders, local Indians attacked Pio Pico's Rancho Jamul near Marron Valley. Pio Pico's ranch foreman, most of his family, and all his servants were killed in the attack. Two of the foreman's teenage daughters were taken away as captives and were never seen again. A third person, supposedly spared by the Indians, was a child between two and three years old named Clara. Although another article said the child's name was Claro, implying the child was a little boy.

According to the report, the attacking Indians were about to end the child's life, when one of the ranch foreman's teenage girls begged them not to kill the baby. She herself was then dragged away. However, the baby's mother was brutally murdered at the scene. Maybe this is the origin of the faceless woman looking for her lost child?

We may never know.

You Be the Judge

At the south end of Marron Valley there are two naturally elevated helicopter landing pads a mile or two apart—one in the middle and one on the west side of the valley, about 300 feet or so high.

On this particular swing shift evening, Tony and I were both assigned to go sit on one. From the landing pads, two agents could overlook and control the entire area. At least, until dark, that is. Once the sun went down, all bets were off. There was no scope, no sensors, and no backup to assist in the event of trouble. Furthermore, the Mexican side was crawling with bandits—not the kind of bandit that occasionally passed through, but the kind that lived there all the time. They stayed out of our view by hiding deep in the woods on the south side of the border, but could easily see our position from their hideouts. So, at sundown, we left our helo-pads and teamed up for safety.

Tony had just recently transferred over from the Imperial Beach Station and was new to Brown Field. He was several years senior to me in the Patrol, but it was his first time working in Marron Valley and the first time he and I had ever worked together in the field. Tony wanted to know more about the history of the area, so we decided to hike down to the old abandoned ranch house near of the mouth of Mine Canyon. It is located between the two helo-pads and almost on the Mexican border itself, so we were already close.

I explained that it was the same house where the last ranch foreman who had lived there was murdered and stuffed down the well either by Mexican bandits or smugglers. Some versions of the story include his family in the attack. Which version is true, I do not know. Either way, the tale was intriguing. Tony was interested, so we headed down to have a look.

We parked about half a mile away from the ranch house and approached carefully on foot, using the trees and bushes as much as possible to get in undetected. There was always the possibility of running into some very unpleasant folks in that area of the border, so we each brought along a short-barreled twelve-gauge shotgun for added protection. After making it down to the abandoned building without incident, we looked around at all the things left behind by the previous occupant. It appeared that after the foreman was murdered, nobody came to claim much, if any, of his belongings. There was a considerable amount of personal things left lying around, as if the house was still occupied. So much so, that it appeared his family may, indeed, have lived there with him when he was murdered.

Some of the agents who had worked the region longer than I claimed that the ranch foreman and, yes, his entire family were murdered that night, going on to say that all of them had been shoved down the well. The murder happened sometime during the 1970s or 1980s, as I mentioned, but I have been unable to find the exact account of this particular one. It is not uncommon for crimes so close to the border to be under reported or even totally ignored at times. Therefore, the lack of easy to find information is not entirely surprising. It does make sense though, and there certainly was plenty of evidence that the man's family was there with him at the time of his murder. If the family was present and, in fact, was killed alongside him, this could be a potential origin of the little girl in white. Nevertheless, it was always weird to see a house that must have once been so full of life become so desolate, eerie, and abandoned. What was once a family's home was now just a sad memory.

We looked around a while longer, but eventually made our way back out. After we hiked some four or five hundred yards away from the ranch house, an extremely bright light hit us both from behind. It was just a flash, but it lit up the entire area ahead of us like it was daylight and then went dark again. Oddly enough, I do not remember it casting our shadow ahead of us. The intensity of its brightness was truly impressive—far too bright to be any sort of flashlight. Furthermore, it seemed to have originated at ground level just a few feet behind us. Whatever the source, we knew that it was definitely not a friendly encounter—human or otherwise.

We both took cover and waited for whatever it was to appear or make a move, but nothing happened. I had brought along a pair of binoculars to use as a form of night vision, since we did not have a night scope in our area, and used them to look for the light source. I was concerned that someone might be trying to advance on us or surround our position. Both of us were, because we knew anyone who would dare illuminate us like that certainly had bad intentions.

Tony and I were positive someone was trying to get the drop on us; yet, after searching the area and coming up empty, I began to wonder if the perp might have run away. Throughout the entire visit to the old house, we had not heard anybody nearby, coming or going. We used our own flashlights to search the brush around us, but there was nobody hiding and no sign that anyone but us had been in the area.

Finally, we turned our lights off again and looked back towards the ranch house with the binoculars. At first, Tony and I both saw lights down at the abandoned dwelling and thought perhaps bandits had come up to the old place after we left. That would have been very odd, though. I have never seen bandits use flashlights before, especially when they knew law enforcement was around.

About then, we noticed that the lights we were seeing were not casting a beam on anything or illuminating any solid objects, nor were the lights being used in a sweeping motion, like one would expect with a flashlight. As I watched through the binoculars, I noticed how erratically the lights moved, like they were dancing around in the air just a few feet off the ground. Tony saw them too, and we watched them for quite some time before they finally faded away.

When strange things happen, it is always a lot more fun when there is someone else to share it with. It is rarely as cool when experienced alone. As much as we enjoyed watching the tiny light show down at the old ranch house, though, we were still quite baffled about the bright light cast from behind us. Hard as we tried, we never did figure out the source of that flash. It was not heat lightning or regular lightning, nor could it have been headlights from a car. It had been far too bright to be from a flashlight or a vehicle's headlamps.

So I ask the reader: Was it paranormal or just some easily explained thing we simply overlooked? It has been years since that night and neither of us has ever figured it out.

Chapter 11
The Big Splash
We Heard But Did Not See

Possibly the strangest experience I ever had during my Border Patrol career happened while I was still on the Field Training Unit. I do not remember the exact date, but it was late February or early March 1995. Three of us and a Field Training Officer were working the midnight shift and headed out to Otay Lakes to work a sensor. We entered the area through a locked gate called the Riding and Hiking Gate on Otay Lakes Road, which restricted public access to the area. We drove through the gate and took a dirt road that led to the backside of the lake. It was the first time we had ever been there.

Along the way, we passed Jeb, one of the Patrol Group A supervisors. Jeb, possibly the best scope operator in the Border Patrol, said he was going to set up a scope and work that area for the night. He was waiting for some traffic expected to come down from the KOA ridgeline later in the shift.

I also remember about that same timeframe a member of the military arrived with a prototype for a new scope. He and one of our supervisors tried it out together. I cannot remember for sure if it was the same night as the following incident, but I believe it was.

The three of us and our training officer continued on another mile or so, until we reached our destination just southeast of Otay Lake. The part of the lake we were working that night had recently burned in a wildfire. The ground and surviving trees were completely covered in black soot. A heavy fog had rolled in on top of that and it looked like something out of a horror movie. It had a very eerie feel to it.

Funny thing about fog is that, while it is only possible to see a short distance, the visible part is very bright and can be seen quite clearly. In heavy fog, it would sometimes be possible to read a book even at midnight without any use of a light. This was one of those nights.

On the training unit, they liked to hike us around as much as possible, so we had parked quite a ways off the trail we intended to work. As we were walking, something really funny happened.

We got lost!

Well, not completely lost. We knew we were on the backside of the lake and south of the Otay River. We were walking parallel to a dirt road and a small tributary feeding the south end of the lake, but we had no clue where the trail was that we were trying to get to. The training officer tried in vain to re-orient us to the proper path, but we just continued to parallel the creek west towards the lake.

Suddenly, without warning, there was a very loud crash in the creek. It did not sound like people running through it, as there were no follow up splashes or disturbances, but more like some exceptionally large object had fallen from the sky. It made a single, but very loud, splash right in the middle of the water and effectively attracted everyone's undivided attention.

While out on foot during night operations, it is critical to stay absolutely silent. We all looked directly to the training officer, but not a word was spoken. We just knew to head towards the creek. As we got closer, everyone could sense something was wrong. The area developed a very bad feel to it. I had never experienced a feeling quite like that before. I was convinced we were about to see something horrible, and I mentally braced myself for whatever we were about to encounter.

More than that, the single splash made no sense. When people, whether a group or a single person, crossed water, it made a distinctive continuous splashing sound. We had heard this many times before and knew exactly what it sounded like.

This was different.

The bad feeling I had developed deepened into a strong foreboding, and I started to feel a powerful sense of dread and intense sadness. This I felt not for myself, but for whatever was in the water. Our small group had been working on night shifts for months and, as a team, we had caught hundreds if not thousands of aliens. We were used to hiking around in canyon bottoms and ridge tops all night long, every night, sometimes in total darkness. Our training officer had several years' experience, yet he too started to feel very uneasy. As a trainee, you are very careful about needlessly drawing a firearm, but I had a very tight grip on mine, as did all the others, including the training officer. His gun was already drawn and aimed toward the creek. It was very unusual that an agent would draw a weapon when accompanied by three others, especially before a particular danger was identified. For some reason, everyone felt the need to do so now, long before we reached our destination.

The four of us arrived at the water's edge and could clearly hear something moving in the creek, though we did not yet have a visual.

There were four or five coyotes, of the canine variety, also present at the scene. Now coyotes normally cry, yelp, and raise quite a ruckus when something intrudes into their turf. We call them a PA's best friend, because they often alert nearby agents when groups of aliens are passing close by. Right now, they were all silent. As a matter of fact, they looked just plain scared. I also noticed, all of the animals were dry. None of them had been in the water, so something else had made that splash.

There were coyotes all along the creek bank, only they were moving away from its edge. It was as if they had been curious about whatever fell into the water, but now wanted nothing to do with it. Most of them appeared to have their ears pinned back and their tails tucked between their legs and were all looking back over their shoulders towards the creek as they were leaving the area. They walked right between the other agents and myself as they passed, but didn't seem interested at all that we were there. The coyotes were so afraid of whatever was in the water, that we didn't even exist.

After the single entry splash, there were no more sounds heard that would indicate something leaving the creek. We knew that whatever had hit the water was still there in the midst of it. We cut for sign all up and down the creek bank, but there was none to be found anywhere. Nothing going in, and nothing coming out. Visibility was such that we could easily see all the way across the water to the other side of the creek, but saw nothing there. We tried using our flashlights, but, because of the fog, the light kept reflecting back into our eyes. They were useless, so we turned them back off.

In the quiet, we could still hear something moving through the water. It actually sounded like someone walking right up the middle of the creek against what little current there was. It definitely was moving to the east away from us, directly into the view of the scope Jeb had set up about a mile away.

I do not know whether the others were hearing the movement or not. My hearing has always been very sensitive. For example, later that night in a completely different area, I heard a group of aliens up ahead of us that none of the other team members heard at all. The Training Officer even asked me if I was sure that I heard a group nearby, because no one else had heard them.

"I am sure of it," I said.

So, we sprinted forward and caught about seven or eight illegals as they were coming down off an eight-foot fence, validating my listening skills. I often heard traffic that others did not hear until they were much closer, so I trusted my ears.

Figure 12—The section of creek/river near our encounter.

Figure 13—The creek/river as it runs east towards the Riding and Hiking Gate.

We continued searching the creek bank and the water in the direction I heard movement, but we never found or saw anything offering us any clue as to the massive splash. After a while, we chalked it up to some weird anomaly and hiked toward the lake to continue our initial patrol.

Later that night, one of the other trainees privately asked me, "What do you think that was in the water?"

"I don't know," I replied, "but I was getting some really bad vibes back there."

"Yeah, I know," he said. "The hair all over the back of my neck was standing straight up."

As far as I know, those were the first and last words ever spoken of that incident by any of us present at the scene. Since the other trainee asked me what I thought it was in the water, I assume that he heard the same movement in the creek that I did. After that, though, it was spoken of no more.

The Eight Foot Tall Mountain Lion

I probably would have forgotten about it entirely if something else had not happened a short time later that same shift—something that caused me to always remember the events at that creek. Later that night, there was another incident close to the Otay River not far from the Riding and Hiking Gate that, at first, seemed to be a separate and unrelated event, although whatever we had just encountered at the creek had headed that direction back to the east. I just barely caught part of the unfolding drama on my walkie-talkie as we hiked on towards the south end of the lake.

Something crazy went down, but I missed most of it. Later the next morning once we arrived back at the station, I asked an agent from another unit if he had heard the entire radio transmission and knew what it was all about. He said that, yes, he had heard it all. The agent then explained what had happened.

Jeb, the supervisor running the scope back down at the Riding and Hiking Gate, had spotted a bunch of illegals. He had called two agents in to work it, and they were out on foot and getting set up. It was a large group coming down off the KOA ridgeline as expected, and they were heading towards Otay Lakes Road. As the agents were moving into position to intercept the illegals, the supervisor suddenly called them off.

The agents were a little reluctant to leave and questioned why they were being called off the group. They could hear the aliens coming and wanted to finish what they had started. Jeb assured them that it was not a group they were hearing but, rather, a very large predator stalking them both. They were instructed to get back to their vehicle immediately and leave the area.

Right away, I started to think that whatever the supervisor Jeb had seen on the scope might be the same thing we had earlier encountered in the creek. Whatever we heard had moved up river back toward the Riding and Hiking Gate. The tributary where our encounter took place also paralleled the road and ran directly into the scope's line of sight. The timing was right as well. It would have taken quite a bit of time to walk that far. The responding PAs heard movement close by, but saw nothing. They merely thought the group of illegals they were expecting to intercept was close by and making the noise. It was almost an instant replay of what had happened to my companions that night, except for one small detail. There was a third party present at the latter scene, and he was running a thermal night scope! That, my friend, casts a whole new light on things, as I would later find out.

The following night during muster, the Field Operations Supervisor gave everyone a very stern warning about operating on foot at night. "You had better watch your backs and be very aware of your surroundings," he said. He then went on to tell us what Jeb had seen near the Otay River the night before while operating the thermal.

"A large predator was seen stalking two PAs while they were working the KOA traffic at Otay Lakes," he informed the patrol group. "It was probably a mountain lion or something, but if it was, it was the largest we have ever seen."

This was the talk of the station for several days before the novelty of it faded away. Everyone assumed it was just a cat, although the FOS was careful not to actually say that it was. I thought that was the end of the story, but it was not!

About a year or so later, Jeb transferred to another agency somewhere back east. As they often do, he told a story or two before leaving. I was not present when he was extrapolating on the previously described event, but an agent who was there passed it on to several of us later.

One night four or five agents, myself included, were sent to the Jamul area to wait for a large group of aliens expected to come down off the mountain. As we were all standing around waiting to receive our plan of action, a BS session broke out. During the session, John, one of the agents present at Jeb's telling, suddenly blurted out, "Did you ever hear what Jeb saw on the night scope at Otay Lakes?"

One of the agents asked, "Do you mean the night he saw a mountain lion following two PAs?"

John laughed. "No! That was all a bunch of bull. It was just a cover story," he told us. "Jeb called in a couple of PAs to work a group coming down off The KOA. The agents had gotten out on foot and were moving in on them when something came up from the river and started stalking the agents. It wasn't a mountain lion like they told us the next night at muster. It was bipedal and walking upright on two feet! When the beast walked up behind the PAs, its size became apparent. It dwarfed both of the agents. It towered over them!" he explained. "Jeb said it was much larger than any bear could have been. It walked like a man, and its heat signature on the scope was massive. Jeb said he had never seen anything like it before."

Yet, the two agents involved in the incident were somehow entirely unaware of its presence. All the while, they were thinking the noise was from a group over a hundred yards away, when it was a beast following right behind them! Now my own bizarre experience at the creek that same night started to make more sense. My opinion about the possibility of Bigfoot creatures and what they really are changed drastically after that evening.

A short time later, Albert, a fellow agent, told me that he had heard the very same story by a different source. The story he knew also involved Jeb witnessing an incredibly large bipedal creature following two agents near the river at Otay Lakes. Albert insisted the sighting was real and that the story was not bogus.

This was not the only possible sighting concerning a Bigfoot or Sasquatch-type creature. I have no personal firsthand knowledge of the following accounts—these were relayed to me by third parties—but they are interesting, so I will share them with you.

Apparently, there was an incident in which a PA working Otay Mountain was walking illegals back to his truck when they, too, were briefly pursued by some type of creature. The agent had caught a small group of four or five illegals shortly before sunset and was leading them back up the mountain on foot to his patrol vehicle. He began to hear brush breaking down below him and, at first, thought it was another bunch of illegal aliens coming up behind him. Then the captured aliens hiking alongside him suddenly became very anxious and tried to get behind the agent.

"Oficial," they said. "Mira eso!" (Officer, look at that!)

Where they pointed, there was some kind of beast walking up the mountain. It was coming towards them, beating the brush in front of it down with its arms in a somewhat swimming motion as it walked. The agent thought the brush to be about six or seven feet high; the beast's head and shoulders were above it. Everyone started to run, including the agent. When they finally stopped and looked back again, the beast was gone.

While working Mine Canyon a different night, a junior agent who had been assigned to ride with me, told me about a group of aliens he had caught in Mine Canyon earlier that month. He said, "The aliens asked me for a favor."

"Yeah, what was that?" I asked.

"They said there was a monster down in the canyon and asked, 'Why don't you go down there and kill it?'" he told me.

Another group of aliens on the west side of the mountain also claimed to have been chased down a trail by a beast in Windmill Canyon.

"I could feel its hot breath," one exclaimed fearfully. "He was breathing down onto the back of my neck!"

141

As usual, the apprehending agents just laughed it off, but the aliens didn't find it humorous. They were serious.

One Big Happy Family

It seems that Brown Field was not the only place with a "monster" running loose. Mark, a friend and fellow agent, told me about a PA he knew at the Campo Border Patrol Station whose hobby was following Bigfoot tracks in their area of operations. Evidently, there was a monster around the Lake Moreno region that the agents referred to as "Little Foot."

Certainly, tracks can be faked if someone wants to play a joke, but they are not likely to fool an experienced Border Patrol agent and the Campo Station had some pretty good trackers back then. I thought the subject was interesting, so I did a little search to see if I could find anything on the Internet concerning the matter. Sure enough, there were stories posted by an anonymous supposed Border Patrol agent from the Campo Station.

The poster claimed that they had indeed found tracks around Lake Moreno and other areas and followed them on several occasions. One of the creatures he referred to as "Little Foot." It was also interesting to note the description of the tracks. As the poster said, one could plainly see sign in the dust made by the hair between the toes. To me that statement was significant.

I have spent a pretty fair amount of time tracking throughout my career and am considered to be quite proficient at it. So, I know it is possible for the hair in between a creature's toes to leave sign on the ground, and any good agent could easily read it. It is also something a tracker likely would not find on fake footprints. Real footprints also dig into the ground a certain way, not to mention the length of stride. Things that fake footprints could not easily match in such detail.

I believe the anonymous poster of that story was indeed a Border Patrol agent who knew what he was talking about. The poster also said the tracks often disappeared without rhyme or reason, even in areas where the tracks should have still been quite easy to follow. Implying that when they feel pressured, they are able somehow to just vanish.

One evening, I was working on top of the mountain near Buttewig Canyon when I encountered several Bureau of Land Management employees on one of the firebreaks. They were the environmentalist types, not law enforcement officers, and we talked for quite a while about the mountain and the wildlife that called it home. It was rare to see these people up there, so I asked what had brought them up that particular evening. They said they had come up to look for bear scat.

I showed my ignorance and asked, "What is bear scat?" I had never heard manure and droppings called scat before. Silly me!

I told them I had been all over the mountain but had never seen any sign for bear. To my knowledge, no other agent had ever claimed to see a bear or discovered sign for one, either. If there was a bear up there, we would know about it. Our people hiked every inch of that mountain on a regular basis. Besides, it seemed rather counterproductive to me to wait until evening to start looking for bear poop.

So just for the fun of it, I asked what they thought about the possibility of a Sasquatch being up there. I kinda chuckled, not wanting them to think I was a nut or something, but their reply surprised me a little bit because nobody laughed. They didn't think it was funny at all. In fact, they thought there could be as many as three of them traveling through the Otay Mountain Range.

They were very explicit, stating they believed there were two adults and a juvenile. I expected them at any moment to break out into laughter at my expense and say they were just kidding, but they never did. They were serious!

Hmm. A juvenile sounds just like "Little Foot" at Lake Moreno, I thought to myself.

After talking with the BLM people that night, I actually started to take the phenomenon more seriously and did a little research on some other sightings. At this point, I do not believe a Sasquatch will ever be captured. I don't think it is an actual creature as we know it or that it normally lives here

143

among us. I think, perhaps, that it is from a different dimension. Humans have found and caught nearly every creature on this planet, yet nobody can catch this one—the biggest of all! Surely, these creatures must have something else going for them. They are huge and not that sneaky. People see them all the time. Instead, I wonder if this being can come and go as it pleases in and out of our dimension, somehow controlling its visibility and, therefore, its vulnerability. Maybe that is why it can be heard or seen on a thermal scope, but rarely with the naked eye.

Who knows?

When Sir Edmund Hillary first encountered the Yeti on his expedition to the Himalayas, he noted, "They seem to go in and out of visibility at will."

I believe this to be true. Therefore, I believe there will always be legitimate sightings, but nobody will ever be able to catch one. Native Americans have always claimed that Sasquatches have the ability to hypnotize people and put thoughts into their heads, thereby causing humans not to see them. I can almost believe it. That night by the river, I remember how strange I felt. Thinking back, it did rather seem as if some outside force had attempted to manipulate my thoughts or make me feel a certain way. My mood had changed against my will and felt beyond my control. Perhaps we were all hypnotized, and that is why we all saw nothing.

I do not know. It sounds great, I suppose, but I am not sure I'm ready to believe all that just yet.

Still, it sure seemed like those coyotes saw something. Whatever it was, they didn't like it because they certainly were not hanging around. Anyway, if this being actually does exist, it is far more advanced than just some big overgrown forgotten monkey or ape-man. I do not believe it is any form of primate at all.

In 1890, Teddy Roosevelt wrote in his book *The Wilderness Hunter* about a Bigfoot encounter called The Bauman Story. So, if I am crazy for relaying these stories and events to you, then at least I am in good company!

If you search long enough, you may eventually see one and perhaps even have an encounter, but, if I am right, you will never get proof.

Chapter 12

Big Cats

Wait...Let Me Get My Gun

I n my twenty-year career, there was only one time that I was ever really scared. Fortunately, it only lasted a few seconds, but it was enough to change the way I operated for the rest of my career.

On a midnight shift during mid-winter, I had a young trainee riding with me and the two of us were assigned to the Otay Lakes area. Around three or four in the morning, a sensor in our area hit. We were close by and moved quickly into position to intercept. The trainee was quite excited about the chance to "bust a group," but he had very little experience, so I decided not to separate from him, such as with our normal north/south maneuver. I wanted this trainee to stay close by.

After twenty minutes or so, we heard something in the brush up on the hillside. At first I thought it might be the aliens, but realized it was much too quiet to be people, so I assumed it was a deer. Ignoring it, we continued to wait.

It was a cold night, and I was wearing a coat, leather gloves, and a bulletproof vest. The ballistic vest was a hand-me-down and much too large for me, so parts of it protruded out to the side. Money was tight at the time, and I could not afford to buy a vest that fit me properly. Still, a vest is a vest, right?

Because of a new Border Patrol policy, I had recently been forced to turn in my revolver and had instead been issued a new semi-automatic pistol. The holster that came with it fit very tightly against the body. I didn't really care for the new sidearm, but that is what the agency had issued, so that's what I had.

Though there had been no movement and no more sounds, my trainee partner and I continued waiting. Then, without warning, from directly behind us came a terrifying scream. I spun around, moving faster than I ever had in my life. In the moonlight, the trainee and I could see an adult mountain lion running right at us!

I grabbed for my weapon but, because of the leather gloves, I got a bad grip and could not get it out. Next, because of the ill-fitting bulletproof vest protruding abnormally to my side and the close position of the new holster against my body combined with the thick winter coat I was wearing, my new pistol got hung up. It was hopelessly stuck, with half the gun still in the holster. With all my might, I tried to tear the gun free, but it was no use.

I shouted at the trainee, "Shoot him! Shoot him!"

But, I heard no gunshots. All I could think of was that I was going to die with my gun in my hand without ever firing a single shot. As far I as could tell, the trainee had also not unholstered his weapon, though I did not know why.

Remember what I said before about luck?

As it turned out, the trainee and I were not the cat's target. Its prey was very near where we were standing—maybe ten or fifteen feet away. The cat came within a few feet of us and then suddenly changed directions and increased his speed.

Whatever the lion was after tried to run for it, but was not fast enough.

We heard a scream even more terrifying than the first. The mountain lion had caught his prey and, mere feet from where we stood, was viciously ripping it up and tearing it to pieces—a truly horrifying sound.

About now, I was finally able to free my weapon and get to a flashlight. It is funny how such little tasks become so difficult under such extreme stress. I shined the light around, but the lion was gone. I didn't have to talk long to convince the trainee it was time to go. He was ready. We were both more than a little shaken.

Neither one of us had heard that cat while it was moving in, stalking its victim. And that last scream we witnessed on the hillside was a combination of the lion and its prey. It was a sound I would not soon forget.

After that night, I completely changed my uniform equipment and gun belt. I dumped the issued holster and bought a "breakaway" that sat slightly away from the body, similar to my previous revolver holster. I took the gloves off and never wore them again either, no matter how cold it got. To this day, I have yet to put a glove back on my gun hand. If it is winter and my hand is cold, I just put it in my pocket for a moment and deal with it.

The very next day, I found the money and bought a brand new ballistic vest custom fitted to me. Replacing all that equipment cost me several hundred dollars I could not really afford, but it was worth every penny. Furthermore, mountain lions became my top safety concern. They always had the drop on humans and, on Otay Mountain, they had definitely lost their natural fear of man. They were always nearby, lurking. It is a miracle that no agent was ever seriously injured or killed by one. It still surprises me to this day.

Eyes of Fire

Sometime around 1998, San Diego Sector started sending agents out to

Arizona on detail. The massive amounts of illegal alien traffic that had once been San Diego's problem was now Arizona's problem. So off we went. About thirty or forty of us reported to the Douglas, Arizona, Border Patrol Station to do for the Tucson Sector what we had done for San Diego Sector. After a day of orientation, I reported for duty the next afternoon for the 3:00 p.m. to 11:00 p.m. swing shift. It was fun to work somebody else's area for a change, and I was looking forward to it.

For the most part, we were sitting on X's, static positions right up against the US/Mexico border fence. Oftentimes, we were sitting in a "war wagon," spending our free time being "rocked" from the Mexican side of the border. A war wagon has expanded metal and a type of cage surrounding the windows of the vehicle so the windows don't shatter in your face when bricks come smashing through. Unfortunately, the metal cage did not always do its job, so I kept an old British army helmet with me to protect my head from rocks and flying glass.

On some X's, it was common to be assaulted multiple times throughout the shift by rocks, bottles, and bricks. I have even seen a few Molotov cocktails thrown over the border fence at agents. On X's, we were acting mainly as scarecrows and were not allowed to leave that position until relieved by the next shift of scarecrows. This freed up more of the local agents who know the area better to work whatever traffic that slipped between the X's. Occasionally, they would give a few detailers, such as myself, a backup position, meaning we were free to go work groups in an assigned area.

One evening, shortly after dark, a detailed San Diego supervisor was working backup when he requested help over his handheld radio. He was working out on foot some distance from his vehicle, was armed with nothing more than a pistol, and had been following a group of illegals cross country.

His progress stopped suddenly, however, when what he believed to be a very aggressive mountain lion blocked his path. The supervisor tried taking a different route, but the cat changed its position and cut him off. The alarmed supervisor re-broadcasted his request for assistance. "This cat is starting to get very aggressive with me," he said.

"We're on our way," local agents radioed. "Where are you?"

Since the detailed supervisor was in unfamiliar territory, he could not tell the local agents exactly where he was, and the cat was becoming increasingly more hostile. The animal was moving in such a way that the stranded agent was unable to see him clearly and could not get a shot off. Every time he tried to escape, the cat growled and cut him off again.

Before long, the supervisor started to get frantic on the radio. His voice cracked, and we could hear the fear in his transmissions. "I need help now!"

"That's a copy. We're looking for you."

"Hurry up," he pleaded, almost in tears. "This cat is very aggressive, and he's not going to let me out!"

Allow me to mention, if you have ever seen the aftermath of a large cat attack, then you would know how justified this man's fear really was.

Fortunately, the ATV team managed to find him and started circling the area, attempting to confuse and distract the big feline. It worked. The animal made a few runs at some of the ATV units, which allowed enough time for another ATV to rush up to the stranded supervisor, pick him up, and get out of there. Later, some of the other detailed agents who knew this particular supervisor well said the man was afraid of nothing. This was the first time they had ever seen him scared.

Well, as luck would have it, the next night I was assigned a backup position. It was very near the area the where the supervisor had worked the night before, and knowing that an aggressive cat was in the immediate area was a little unsettling. Only a week earlier, another PA thought he had seen a bear on one of the trails as well. The bear sighting also proved to be true. I had little faith in our service-issued pistols to deal with such dangerous game, so I took along a shotgun that night. I figured a twelve gauge loaded with slugs should get the job done if the need arose.

Shortly after dark, I was cutting for alien sign on one of the roads and, sure enough, there it was: a whole string of fresh footprints crossing the road. It looked like maybe twenty to twenty-five illegals, and I knew it was less than thirty minutes old, because I had just cut that road half an hour ago and it was clean.

I called dispatch to report the group's crossing location, and let them know I would be out on foot following the sign. It was actually a very bright night, a near full moon, so I was able to follow the sign most of the time without the use of a flashlight. I was making good time too. However, some of the areas with heavy brush were still very dark down on the ground.

About thirty minutes into the tracking operation, I heard a loud thud hit the trail directly behind me, and not the kind of sharp thud a boot or hoofed animal would make. I was in a somewhat remote area, and it was very quiet out, so the sound was clear and distinct. It was heavy but soft, like a pawed animal. Whatever it was, was large and thirty feet behind me.

I spun around like my pants were on fire, but caught only a faint glimpse of something darting into the brush line near a ravine. Of course, my first thought was of the cat from the night before, which is exactly why I had brought the shotgun. I was keeping the weapon leveled on that brush line too!

Fortunately for me, the Douglas Station had numerous infrared night vision cameras set up on high poles all through their area of operations, which were monitored 24/7 back at the control center. I started looking around for one and, sure enough, spotted a camera not too far away. That was a big relief!

I called the control center and told them where I was and that some kind of large animal had come up behind me on the trail. I thought it was in the brush line to my south, and asked them if they could see it.

The control center took a look, but informed me it could not see the animal. However, they did say, "We cannot see in the ravine to your south, it could be down in there."

"Yeah, I'm not going down there to look for it," I replied.

"10-4, Sir," acknowledged the dispatcher that it probably would not be a good idea.

"Can you just watch my back while I try to walk out of here?" I asked.

Dispatch replied, "10-4. Agents are rolling your way to help you out."

I got out of there without any trouble and, within twenty minutes, caught up with the group of illegals. With the aid of the other agents who had come to help, we arrested over twenty people.

Most likely, the cat caught wind of the group and started stalking them, waiting for someone to separate or get left behind. When I came and fell in solo behind the group, it appeared as if I was the one left behind!

The next night, a sensor went off, indicating motion in the same area, but this time there was only silence. Nobody answered it. There were sightings by other PAs as well, but nobody had actually gotten a really good look at the cat, only brief glimpses under the cover of darkness. So Arizona Fish and Game or the Forestry Service, I can't remember which, came out and set up trail cams in the area. Within a few days, they had their culprit. It was not a mountain lion after all. It was a 250 plus pound Jaguar!

Fish and Game said the animal was a young male probably struggling to find enough food and believed he was starting to see people as easier prey.

Well that was certainly a relief! I thought for a night or two that he was just being mean!

A few days later, my detail ended, and I returned back to my home station at Brown Field. Home sweet home.

Chapter 13
Farewell San Diego
Leaving Brown Field

After thirteen years at Brown Field, I decided it was time to move on. Things were getting a little boring. I had just gone through a divorce and the glory days of Brown Field were long past, so a change seemed to be in order.

In September 2007, I transferred to a checkpoint station in Kingsville, Texas. Although the checkpoint had its moments, it was mostly office work and very little fieldwork. In the four years of checkpoint duty, I never experienced even the slightest adrenaline rush and, soon, I began to feel suffocated and longed for the excitement of the west again. So, in October 2011, I transferred to the Tucson, Arizona, Station and closed out my career there.

Figure 14—Baboquivari Peak, southeast of Tucson, AZ.

At Tucson, I felt right at home from the very first day. I was back in the thick of things and could not have been happier about it. I will not bore you with too many heroic war stories, but there was one day that was exceptionally comical.

April Fool's Day 2013 was a fool's day to remember, and boy did it ever live up to its reputation! Fools were running amuck. They were everywhere! Except this was no joke. These fools were for real.

I was assigned the Arivaca Checkpoint along with two other agents and was mostly not involved in the antics of the day. That, however, did not preclude us from enjoying the radio traffic of those who were. Midway through the shift, a call went out from 860 dispatch. It started in the usual way: "Is there an agent who could respond to the town of Arivaca and assist with an accidental shooting in a bar until the Pima County Sheriff's Department is able to arrive? PCSD is enroute."

Any PA with more than a few months in could see this was a giant can of worms just waiting to be opened. Nevertheless, somebody took the bait.

154

Arivaca is a small town with no police force and most of the townfolk like it that way. Although there are many very nice, respectable people who live there, they are often overshadowed by those who are not. The town residents consist of a large number of convicted felons, drug and human trafficking smugglers, crystal meth dealers, and plenty of meth customers. The town is also busy with folks walking to and fro all day long, often with visible firearms sticking out of their pants or in holsters, as is permitted by Arizona law.

Oh, did I mention many of them also hate the Border Patrol?

The first Agents arrived only to quickly discover that this was not an accidental shooting at all. Rather, it was a negligent shooting committed by a convicted felon in a drunken stupor. He had been going around pointing the gun at people inside the bar and threatening to shoot them with it when the weapon went off and struck an older woman in the leg. Some of the local townsfolk were holding the suspect down, while others preferred to assist him by hiding the gun before the Border Patrol Agents and Sheriff's Deputies arrived.

As the BP units attempted to secure the shooter, the remaining townspeople started screaming at and taunting the agents. "Yeah, here comes the federal government with their machine guns, trying to take over our town," they mocked.

When the men holding the suspect down loosened their grip to allow the agents to handcuff him, the shooter decided to make a fight of it. After a little scuffle, one of the agents pepper sprayed the suspect and then placed him in cuffs. Of course, this really got local knuckleheads riled up. At that point, no one really cared about the innocent woman who had been shot or the other five people the drunken perp had threatened with his gun, nor did the local yahoos care that the shooter was drunk or that he had weed in his pocket. It did not matter that he was not legally allowed to have a gun in the first place, being a convicted felon. The only thing that mattered was "Border Patrol is in our town, and we don't want them here."

Of course, a heartfelt thanks is always appreciated!

While the rest of us were enjoying all that radio traffic, our checkpoint was graced with the presence of another resident from Arivaca. A woman wanted to make a formal complaint. It seems that the day before, her daughters had driven up to the checkpoint and had been sent to the secondary inspection area. The woman was pleasant enough, but angry that her eighteen and fifteen year old daughters had been detained until a drug K-9 unit could arrive and perform a sniff of the car.

While the girls were detained, an agent asked them a few questions, such as: Is this your car? Where are you going to, coming from, etc.? The woman claimed she had read our service handbook and wanted to inform me that we are not allowed to ask people any questions, except to check for citizenship, of course.

Well, our handbook is a secured item and not available for the public to read. Moreover, she had definitely not read it, as it absolutely does permit and even encourages such questions. We can actually ask anything we think is relevant if we suspect a crime is being committed. Whether a person decides to answer these questions or not, however, is solely up to him or her. So, I gave the women the station's number, bid her good day, and she went on her way. Later on, I learned that we had arrested her husband several times in the past for drug smuggling, validating the detaining agent's concerns over the girls.

Well, the day was nearly over...or so I thought. I was about to learn that April Fool's does not end just because the sun goes down.

As I was driving back to the station at the end of shift, a second call for help by another OA (other agency) was put out over the air. Fortunately, this call was far from my area, but it went something like this:

"This is 860 (dispatch). Is there an agent who can assist the TOPD (Tohono O'odham Police Dept.) on a domestic violence call on the reservation? TOPD is several minutes out."

Of course, our agents were closer. We always were, which is why they called us so much.

I listened as the PAs near the area answered up and arrived at the scene several minutes ahead of TOPD. There was no address for the house, only

Figure 15—That's right. It's a cattle drive. A whole herd marching right through the checkpoint. (Just for fun pics.)

Figure 16—Is that Gill Favor and Rowdy Yates in the back? (Rawhide)

a description. Nevertheless, agents arrived and found a woman with a very serious gash on her head. They called an ambulance immediately, claiming the woman would need at least twenty stitches to close the wound.

As it turned out, her husband had hit her over the head with a crowbar, and then ran out of the house on foot. Once TOPD arrived, they sat with the woman until the ambulance made it. The agents were then free to start tracking down the loving husband, who had taken to the hills in the dark of night.

Unfortunately for him, Border Patrol agents are often pretty good trackers and, when motivated by the plight of an innocent victim, they can also be quite persistent. Even on a dark night, it did not take long for the agents to track him down and drag him from his hiding spot.

Tracking skills should never be underestimated, deemed old fashioned, or considered out of date. Time and time again, I have seen criminals escape or evade local, state police, and even other federal agencies, only to be tracked down by a Border Patrol agent, often to the amazement of all involved, including the perp who erroneously thought he was home free.

The Mexican Standoff

As I was winding this book down, one of the younger guys, Agent Olaya, approached me and asked if he could be included. He knew what the book was about and thought it would be a pretty interesting read, so he wanted to be part of it. I gave him a quick on the spot interview.

"Alright, Mr. Olaya, have you ever seen a ghost while on duty?" I asked.

"No sir," he replied.

"Okay. Perhaps, you have seen a bigfoot."

He shook his head. "Not that either."

"Well, you have at least been abducted by an alien spacecraft while on patrol, right?" I asked, pretending to be serious.

The younger agent laughed. "Nope, not even that."

"Now, Mr. Olaya, how can I possibly put you in my book about the paranormal when all you have done is just normal stuff like shootouts and car chases?"

The weirdness, it seems, has not yet presented itself to Agent Olaya. Nevertheless, I did decide to add a story about him. Fortunately or unfortunately, depending on how you see it, this PA was going through one of those times that nearly every everybody experiences on and off throughout his or her career where it seemed as if trouble was actively seeking him out. It found him, too, on a regular basis, and was on him like a wet shirt. For example:

Olaya would be given the same routine assignments as everyone else. For the other agents, nothing would happen. Olaya would walk in and karma showed up to greet him. For instance, ten patrol units might take the same exit ramp going back to the station at the end of shift and all would be quiet. Agent Olaya would take the same exit ramp five minutes later and a man would suddenly decide to beat his girlfriend, in the middle of the road, right in front of Agent Olaya's patrol unit. Everybody, including Olaya, thought the run of luck that he kept having was pretty funny, until one day things took a serious left turn.

Sasabe, Arizona, switched between hot and cold when it came to action. Lately it had been cold. I had been assigned there several times myself the previous two weeks. There were drag roads there, which were cut for sign twice a shift, along with sensors and cameras. It was hard to get through without being detected by something or someone. Oddly enough, for the last couple of weeks, there had been no action in the area.

The following Sunday, Agent Olaya was assigned to the Sasabe area. All seemed quiet, until the agent was alerted that intruders were present on the U.S. side of the border. Although cameras had a very clear view of the area, they did not report seeing anything, but Agent Olaya went to investigate anyway. Expecting to find nothing more than a stray animal or another false alert, Olaya headed to the area in question alone. He also left his M4 automatic rifle behind. After all, the area had been silent for weeks.

Do you remember what I said about disaster striking on the most mundane of days?

Well, Agent Olaya arrived on scene and began sweeping the area when he suddenly and very unexpectedly came face to face with what appeared to be two Mexican soldiers on the U.S. side of the border.

Everyone went for their weapons at the same time. And there he was, caught in a true Mexican standoff. One U.S. Border Patrol Agent with nothing more than a pistol versus two apparent Mexican soldiers armed with high-powered G3 H&K fully automatic assault rifles with high capacity magazines. With everybody aimed in on everybody else, it was quite a predicament. Fortunately, nobody had fired yet, which was especially good for Agent Olaya, who was outgunned and positioned to get the short end of this one.

Discretion being the better part of valor, the agent recognized an opportunity to get out of this one without gunfire, i.e., getting killed. We have already talked about how poorly pistols fare against rifles on open ground, and the agent was definitely caught on open ground. The cameras should have easily seen the armed intruders and provided ample warning to the agent, but, for whatever reason, they did not.

So Agent Olaya lowered his weapon slightly and asked, "Es militar?" (Are you military?)

One of the two men replied, "Si." (Yes.)

The young agent then pretended as if it were no big deal. "Bueno," he said, and then lowered his weapon a little more.

The soldiers lowered their weapons also.

Next, Olaya casually started walking towards the soldiers, talking to them as if all was well—another very good move, in my opinion. If things went bad, he needed to be as close as possible to give his pistol a chance against their rifles. If he could get inside their hip pocket, he could get into range for his pistol. At the distance they were currently at, his chances were somewhere between slim and none, and slim was getting on a bus to leave town.

A wise old kung fu master once told me, "To find safety, go to the heart of danger."

As the agent closed in, the soldiers started quickly walking back to the border. Agent Olaya asked them their names, and they replied, but when he got close enough to read their name tags, he realized they were lying. The names they gave did not match the ones on their uniforms.

The soldiers made it safely back to the small barbed wire fence separating the U.S. from the Mexican side of the border. Although the matter ended peacefully, it somehow made its way into the news wire, and rightfully so. This is a serious matter, and the American people have a right to know what is really happening on our nation's border.

A watchdog group reported 29 different incursions by Mexican military, police, and other officials since 2006. The group also claimed that Department of Homeland Security records showed more than 200 similar incidents between Mexican officials and U.S. Border Patrol agents. I was still on duty in the area when some of these incursions happened. I assure you, this is accurate.

And that is how Agent Olaya made it into my book about the paranormal, by doing just regular Border Patrol stuff. Because our normal boring stuff is quite paranormal to the average citizen, and more of these stories need to be told. They seldom are, however, and that is a shame.

The UFO Photo Bomb

I have relayed to you, the reader, many extraordinary stories that may be quite hard to believe. As I mentioned before, few if any other non-fiction book concerning law enforcement have ever touched the subject of the supernatural or paranormal. It is taboo to discuss it in the open and is indeed a career killer, which is why I waited until retirement to write this book. If some wish to ridicule me for this now, I do not care. Yet, oddly enough, I have met almost no ridicule from other agents, merely curiosity mixed with a healthy dose of positive support. All the stories I was involved in are true and I have relayed them to the best of my ability. The stories that were passed to me, I have retold to the best of my understanding. I trust the agents who shared them and do not doubt their authenticity.

It stands to reason that if somebody would lie about seeing ghosts and monsters, then he or she would surely lie about other things as well? Have you noticed that there is one kind of story totally missing from this book so far? In the first nineteen years of my career, I never once heard any agent ever claim to have seen a UFO, flying saucer, space alien, or abduction story of any type. I have heard plenty of police reports, news reports, and late night talk radio of such things from local police officers, but never from a Border Patrol Agent. If anyone should have an encounter with a UFO, it should be a Border Patrol Agent.

There are thousands of agents patrolling some of the most remote areas imaginable. They have fantastic views from mountain tops and desert floors, often near military bases, around the clock every night, continuously looking through binoculars and night vision devices of all sorts; yet, there was not a single sighting that I heard of in those first nineteen years.

I am sure that, if UFOs exist, somewhere out there a Border Patrol agent has seen one. I suspect the story just has not made its way back to my ears. Certainly, there is no actual law requiring that agents report such things to me, but it might have made for an interesting chapter. For now, assuming Martians have invaded, the witnessing PAs have decided to keep it to themselves.

Given the fact that I had never heard a serious UFO story from any agent in all those years of working multiple stations in California, Texas, and Arizona gives further credence that the other stories concerning the paranormal are true. Of all stories, UFO sightings are probably the ones most misinterpreted and the most often lied about, but in nineteen years I did not have a single one. Ultimately, it's up to you, the reader, to decide what to believe.

Statistically, most UFO sightings are by and large a mistake in identity and easily explained, though some sightings I believe to be quite legitimate. I am certainly open to that possibility. I just find it strange that Border Patrol agents are not seeing them. After all, ninety percent or more of our job is making visual and auditory observations. Perhaps agents observe the night sky so often that they are easily able to identify what is flying overhead and are not prone to misidentify something another person might mistake as a UFO.

Then again…maybe we have all been abducted by extraterrestrials and our memories were deleted!

Yeah, the wife didn't buy that one either.

In nineteen years, not one UFO story surfaced. In year twenty, however, one did.

News Flash!

During the last year of my career, while writing this book, I finally became aware of a single UFO sighting. A very legitimate sighting, too, I might add! I was almost disappointed because I hate it when a perfect record is broken!

While working at the Tucson Station in 2014, I walked into the muster room shortly before our daily briefing to the buzz of a UFO sighting. The craft was observed quite thoroughly by some of the newer technology, and there were numerous witnesses to the event.

This was the Holy Grail of sightings. Unfortunately…that's all I can say.

Chapter 14
The Cliffs
Terrain That Does Not Forgive

For this section of the book, I have brought the reader back to the beginning of my career. Class 267 had just graduated from the Border Patrol Academy and the Station Training Unit and was now on the Field Training Unit serving with our assigned patrol groups. I was assigned to Patrol Group A, the one patrol group all trainees dreaded going to. Patrol Group A training officers delighted in keeping their trainees under maximum stress at all times, and was by far the most difficult patrol group to be assigned to.

This particular training phase started at the six-month point in a trainee's career and lasted until he or she took their ten-month test. At that time, he or she either passes and becomes an agent or fails and becomes an unemployed citizen once more. Pretty simple and straightforward stuff, right? Almost sounds easy.

The last half of March, the training unit began working Otay Valley and Dam Canyon. There was a lot of traffic going through there, and we were catching hundreds of illegals each night.

Close to Dam Canyon, the terrain became very dangerous. The most dangerous area was the cliffs leading up the side of Otay Dam itself. There were sheer drop offs of 120 feet or more and a very narrow trail between the cliffs and concrete dam. The trail was treacherous and had to be climbed hand over foot. That area was also very, very dark most of the time.

An old supervisor once told about a time he went down into the canyon to work some traffic during a midnight shift. He went down with other agents, but eventually got separated. Radios were nearly worthless down there and communications were horrible near the bottom of the dam. The supervisor was unable to raise his partners on the radio and soon burned out his only flashlight. It was his first time in the area and he was in a pickle. He had no partners, no radio, no flashlight, and he was hopelessly lost.

I asked him, "What did you do?"

He laughed and said, "I got so scared I just hid behind some rocks all night and waited for daylight."

I could sympathize with him. Dam Canyon was a pretty dark and eerie place, not the kind of place someone wanted to get caught in, especially alone at night.

On March 25, 1995, it was just a little after midnight when two other trainees, an FTO, and I arrived at the Otay Lakes Park. Our plan for the shift was to drop into the middle of Dam Canyon and work traffic until daybreak. The four of us needed to get into the bottom of the canyon without using any source of light, as even the smallest glow would alert the illegals to our presence and make it nearly impossible to catch any of them.

It was a very dark night and climbing down the cliffs at the dam was not an option—it was simply too dark to attempt without lights. Our FTO decided instead to take us in from the top of the hill on the south side of the park. It was a steep slope of about 800 feet, but no cliffs. The darkness was such that we had to continually use our binoculars to see each other in order to stay together. We certainly did not want to get lost from the training officer.

Going down, we were constantly slipping and falling. I must have fallen at least five times before it was over, but once we reached the bottom and got set up we had a field day. Other trainees and their FTOs had come into the canyon from different angles and, by morning, we had apprehended almost 300 illegal aliens.

On Sunday, March 26, 1995, we arrived again at Otay Lakes Park just after midnight. Same setup—myself, two different trainees, and the same FTO—but this time the FTO decided that he would not accompany us down into the canyon. He wanted to take a different route and said, "Elmore, since you went down the steep slope on the backside of the hill last night, you will lead the other two trainees down it tonight."

I did not care for the plan. Nonetheless, Ralph, Manny, and I took off downward from the top of the hill with me leading. It was equally as dark as the night before, so we met with pretty much the same results. We all fell about five times apiece, but eventually reached the bottom of the canyon. Once there, it took all of about fifteen minutes for the three of us to catch about sixty illegals.

Then guess what?

We had to walk the crowd back up the hill in total darkness. We had met up with other agents in the canyon, so Ralph stayed at the bottom with them, while Manny and I escorted the sixty back up to the park to wait for transport, walking back up the same way we had just come down. Let me tell you, hiking down an 800-foot hill with a partner is a lot easier than hiking back up it, in the dark, with sixty prisoners in tow.

Obviously, we didn't have sixty pairs of handcuffs, so we had to make do with plastic zip ties, which we called flexi-cuffs. We had enough to hook most of the men together, but there were fifteen or twenty walking on the honor system.

As you can imagine, letting people who have just been arrested tag along without proper handcuffs often leads to spurts of random excitement along the way. Escapes and assaults were the most common, especially when there were only two of us. However, if the cuffing is done properly and the correct people are hooked together, the others will just follow suit.

This particular group was actually pretty cooperative and offered no resistance. Nevertheless, it took a good long while to make all the way back to the top with them. Once we finally reached the park, we had to call for a bus to pick them up because there were far more than we could fit in one or two transport vans. In the canyon bottom, we only had time to pat them down for weapons the best we could so, while we waited, my partner and I thoroughly searched each and every one. The bus finally came and took away the trophies of our labor, but the night was far from over. Already, several other groups were running amuck in the bottom of Dam Canyon.

So, right back down we went.

This time, we met with a snag, though. The battery on Manny's radio died, and he could not receive or transmit. There was a scope in operation at the peak of the hill just above the park. We thought maybe the scope operator might have an extra battery to loan us for the remainder of the shift, so we hiked up to his position and asked.

Nope. No extra battery. However, the scope operator turned out to be Lupe, one of our FTOs, and he informed us that Manny could no longer work traffic. The trainee would have to remain at the scope truck with him, since it was not safe to be out on foot without a walkie. Manny had sworn not to leave my side, but it was no dice. Lupe would not budge.

All alone, I started the trek back down. I was getting to know this dang hill pretty well after going up and down it so many times the last two nights, and I was maneuvering it like a pro. In fact, I spent so much time hiking this bit of terrain that, despite the cold March temperature, I was sweating profusely the entire night.

Most of the time, we spent our shifts doing lay-ins and waiting around for traffic, and it was cold, so everyone wore the heaviest coats and jackets they had. I was wearing a winter coat with a ballistic vest underneath, so between the body armor, the coat, and nonstop mountain hiking, I was soaking wet. That meant every time I stopped to lay-in or work a group, I would freeze.

After I left Manny, I did not get far down the trail before I heard Ricardo, one of the FTOs down in the canyon, going off. He was ticked because the training unit allowed a group to slip past. Now, that group was climbing up a cliff face near the Pipe Crossing, and it was too dangerous for the trainees to follow, so it appeared that bunch was going to get away.

I informed the FTO that I was still near the top and thought I could cut over towards the Pipe Crossing and intercept them.

The FTO said that if I would light up, he would be able to see my light as he was up high and cross canyon from me. But the group was still near enough to the bottom that they would not see the light from their position. By tracking my flashlight as I ran across the top of the canyon, he could put me in position to cut them off, without the group knowing I was there.

Once he saw my light, he said, "Run hard to the west and I'll call your stop, but be careful up there!"

I had not hiked that side before, but I knew there were cliffs and drop-offs there. The scope could not see that area from his position and was unable to help guide me in, so I lit up and ran to the west. It was farther than I thought, but I beat the group to the rendezvous point, shut off the light, and took a sitting position about 150 feet above the cliff. I scanned the cliff top with a pair of binoculars, hoping to see a head pop up. I did not have to wait long. The first head popped into view and its owner crawled across the top of the cliff, then another and another. Eventually, the whole group of seventeen was on top and ready to take flight. They had run from the agents at the bottom of the valley and clearly did not intend to stop for anyone. After huddling up for a moment, they all got up and raced toward me at full speed.

I waited for them to get close before I sprang from my position. "Sientense todos!" I shouted.

Lot of good that did! Quick lesson: It is hard to stop a group once they start running.

Upon seeing me, the illegals immediately turned and ran back to the east. I had hoped this would be easy, but no such luck. Initially, I had no intention of chasing people around in the dark up there by myself, though that is exactly where this was headed.

As I started after them, I looked up and saw a very welcome sight. Manny was running my way from the east—Yes!—with the aliens sandwiched between us! When the sprinters saw him, they turned, looked at me again, and then just sat down.

We got all seventeen of them.

"What are you doing here?" I asked Manny. "Lupe said you had to stay with him at the truck."

"Lupe told me to hurry up and get over here," he explained. "He thought it was more dangerous for you to work this group alone than for me to be without a radio."

After we wrapped the bunch up, the night was nearly over—none too soon, either, because I was whooped. At the end of the night, I was weak and exhausted. The last few nights working the Dam Canyon area had been chaos, so by the end of shift Sunday morning, March 26, I felt like I was catching the flu. I had chills and could not stop shaking from the cold. All the hiking up and down the canyon wall and alternating between sweating and cooling had taken its toll.

I told you the story about working in Dam Canyon not to mesmerize you with my superb alien catching abilities but, rather, to set up what happened Tuesday morning, March 28, 1995, just one or two minutes after midnight.

I was scheduled to be Border Patrol Agent (Trainee) Luis Santiago's partner for the midnight shift, March 28, and was looking forward to it. Originally from Puerto Rico, Luis had a good sense of humor and those around him were always laughing. He was a natural comedian and very likable, but was always extremely safety conscious. He wore his bulletproof vest everywhere he went, even on days we were just attending classroom activities.

I had never been paired up to work with Santiago before, and I was certain it would be an interesting night. Like I said, I was looking forward to it. Even better, it was only two or three days before our final test as trainees, the "ten month exam." If we passed it, we would be real agents. If we failed, we were fired. Either way, this would be one of our last nights in the field as trainees.

Since Monday was a "Post Academy Day" for Patrol Group A trainees, we would have an extra eight hours of rest before reporting for classroom training Monday morning at seven, but there was a catch. The eight hours of rest we gained Sunday, we lost Monday. Once Post Academy training was over at four o'clock Monday afternoon, we had to go straight home, grab what little sleep we could, and then report to the station before eleven o'clock for the midnight shift.

The extra eight hours of rest did me no good. When I arrived at class Monday morning, I felt worse than the day before. I struggled to get through the day and was wondering how I would ever get through the upcoming shift later that night with a maximum of five hours sleep. During our lunch break, most of the class was standing outside BS-ing and telling what few war stories they had when Santiago voiced his concern about working up on the mountain. He was worried about groups turning on the agents and not being able to get backup in time.

I believe his exact words were, "If you run into a group of twenty by yourself and they jump you, you're just dead and that's it!"

Santiago naturally had a funny way of saying things and everyone laughed at his comment. Nobody was overly worried about getting jumped, but we all knew how safety conscious he was, so it just seemed funny.

Santiago had been a San Diego County Sheriff's Deputy before joining the Border Patrol, so he did know what he was talking about, and I had no doubt that working with him that night was going to be a riot!

After class ended for the day, I immediately went home and tried to sleep. However, when I awoke that evening and got up to prepare for work, I couldn't manage. I felt worse than before and there was no ignoring it. I was sick. The FTOs had warned us that as trainees we had better not call in sick, but I knew that to work the Dam Canyon area I needed to be a hundred percent. A sluggish agent could get hurt very quickly out there. Reluctantly, I called the station, spoke with a supervisor, and "banged in" eight hours' sick leave.

I will never know how fateful this decision may or may not have been.

Now, my absence did not leave Santiago without a partner. There were several other agents assigned the same general area, and Santiago was assigned to work with an FTO named Mikey and two or three other trainees.

After calling in sick, I put my equipment—gun belt, baton, radio, and firearm—back on a shelf in the closet and went back to bed. I was asleep within minutes. A little while later, however, I was woken by a beeping sound. It had a rhythm to it, like a distress signal.

I was unsure where it was coming from and stumbled around in the dark a few moments until I could locate the source. Eventually, I realized it was coming from my equipment in the closet. More specifically, it was coming from my service issued radio, yet I was positive it had been turned off before it was put away.

I checked and, indeed, it was off, but the beeping from the radio continued. I supposed the battery had a short. I turned the radio on and then back off again. It beeped a few more times and then finally stopped.

As I climbed back in bed, I noticed the clock. It read 12:02—just after midnight. Almost instantly, I went back to sleep.

The next morning I felt much better, so much so that I even went out and had pancakes for breakfast. I returned home about ten o'clock in the morning and found a message waiting on my answering machine. It was my cousin Darryl, a San Diego County Deputy. He sounded very worried and said I needed to call him immediately to let him know that I was alright.

Puzzled, I gave him a ring, "Hey, I'm fine. What's up?"

Darryl told me the awful news. A Border Patrol trainee had been killed the night before at Otay Lakes Dam, right at midnight, two days short of his ten-month test. My class. My shift. The news media had not released the name of the agent yet, and he was worried that it might have been me.

I was stunned.

One of my classmates was dead, and, despite the academy's best efforts to prevent it, I was friends with all of them. I wondered which one, but didn't really want to know. I knew the station would be chaotic, so I did not dare call. Instead, I called Tim, another one of my classmates, and prayed he would answer the phone. After a couple of rings, he answered. It was a partial relief only because that meant it was somebody else.

We didn't waste time with small talk.

"Who was it?" I asked.

"Santiago," he answered.

Neither of us felt like talking. I hung up the phone, stunned.

When I reported for duty that night, the station was nearly empty. There was one or two supervisors, one Field Training Officer, one regular agent, and most of Luis Santiago's classmates from Patrol Group A. Everyone else had called in for leave and stayed home.

The Supervisor stood up and addressed muster by saying, "It's nice to see that at least some of you have a sense of duty."

I knew exactly what he meant. When someone is killed on duty, the agents of that station have an option to stay home from work. It is like a mental health day to help recover from the trauma or to comfort their families. This is probably deducted from sick leave, but I wouldn't know because I never exercised that option.

What the supervisor meant by his comment, however, was that the regular agents and other supervisors should have reported for duty that night, since they had not worked with the deceased agent and did not really know him. Luis Santiago's classmates were the individuals that should have stayed home in order to recoup their thoughts and feelings, but we were all there. I felt it was my duty to be there for my classmate, no matter how I felt.

Next, we were all given the official explanation of what had happened the night before.

The training unit had arrived at Dam Canyon shortly before midnight, just like they had previous nights. Just as before, there were already groups in the bottom of the canyon waiting to be worked. Santiago was assigned to work with his Training Officer Mikey and two or three other trainees. One of our other classmates, Alan, was running the scope from the top of the park that night. A group was detected trying to climb up the trail in between the Otay Lakes Dam and the cliffs adjacent to it. The illegals evidently heard the agents coming and retreated back to the bottom of the canyon.

The training unit was near the top of the dam already, and their FTO started leading them down the trail towards the bottom. For some reason, Santiago decided to stay up top, near the dam and next to the cliffs. Whether he saw aliens already on top of the cliff, I do not know. The scope operator had spotted a group somewhere in the general area, though, and Santiago was talking to him about it over the radio.

Suddenly, he ran towards the cliff, telling the scope operator, "I'll be there in a minute!"

Those were the last words he ever spoke.

Next, there was a loud scream. The trainees and their FTO Mikey saw Luis's flashlight tumble down the cliff and knew immediately what happened.

Mikey frantically called the other FTO on the radio. "An agent just fell off the dam!"

Ricardo, the other FTO, asked, "Off the north side?" meaning into the water, where it was survivable.

"No, "Mikey answered back, "the south side!"

Everyone knew what that meant.

When the others reached the bottom of the cliff face, they found Luis Santiago's body. He had fallen 120 feet to the rocks below and nothing could be done. He was already dead. A Field Operations Supervisor arrived on scene, and made the one call no agent ever wants to hear over the radio.

"The agent is 10-7."

All rescue efforts ceased and the scene immediately turned to an investigation. Investigators ultimately ruled it an accident, claiming he had simply fallen off the cliff ledge while running. I do not think most of his classmates ever believed that. I know that I certainly didn't.

Why had he gone up there to begin with? Had he seen somebody that the others had not?

Ultimately, that was the official explanation. The time of death was estimated at around 12:01 or 12:02 a.m., Tuesday morning, March 28, 1995. The memorial was held later that week on Friday. It was the first time I had ever attended a funeral for a fallen officer or agent. It was impressive and emotional.

Before joining the Border Patrol, I had been in private business. One of my customers was a trumpet player for the U.S. Army's Honor Guard, and his job was to play Taps at military funerals. Once he told me, "You always know when you play it right, because when you hit the third note, they all start to cry."

He was right: they did.

On that day, I heard for the first time a song even more heartbreaking. I had heard "Amazing Grace" sung in the Lord's Church all my life, but never on the bagpipes at a fallen agent's funeral before. It was the most gut-wrenchingly beautiful song I have ever heard.

A few weeks earlier, two FBI agents had come to our training facility to give us a talk about corruption. The entire academy class of 267 attended, including Luis Santiago. I remember two things they said very distinctly. One of them said, "Don't worry about getting killed on duty. It's not going to happen. You should worry instead about corruption or getting caught taking a bribe, because then we will arrest you and put you in prison," he warned. "I guarantee that none of you in this room will ever get killed on duty."

I guess you know now what an FBI guarantee is worth. We were not even off the training unit and, already, I was attending the funeral of a friend, a classmate, a fellow agent.

The night of the memorial service, I went to bed around 10:30. It had been a hard day, and I was sleeping soundly until I woke to a rhythmic beeping coming, again, from my closet. I opened the door and found my work radio going off in the same weird rhythm as the other night. I looked at the clock and it read 12:02 a.m.

The hair on my neck lifted.

I had an overwhelming feeling that someone was waiting for me to press the talk button and say something, but I did not have the courage. I was afraid who might answer back. I double-checked the radio to make sure it was off, and it was. I turned it on and off a couple of times, as before, but it continued to beep. Finally, I took the battery off and it stopped. I carried that radio on duty for years after that night. The only time it ever beeped like that was the night of Luis Santiago's death, and the night of his memorial service.

The next week at work, I asked some of the more senior agents about the distress signals our radios could make. They told me our radios were not capable of sending distress signals. There were no emergency buttons or beeping rhythms on our radios at that time.

Figure 17—To the right is the slope we hiked down in order to avoid the cliffs at the Otay Dam and Pipe Crossing.

Figure 18—Top of the Pipe Crossing where Manny and I arrested the group of seventeen that had climbed up the cliffs.

Figure 19—The cliff that took Luis Santiago's life. Distance is a little deceiving. It does not look like a 120 foot drop, but it is.

Figure 20—Top view from the cliff. Can you see the drop off?

Figure 21—Memorial to Luis Santiago. Otay Lakes Dam can be seen in the background.

Figure 22—Border Patrol Agent Luis Santiago, an American hero.

Chapter 15
The Reappearance Of Luis Santiago
It Began with Hate Speech

I t is with very mixed feelings and a bit of hesitation that I tell the rest of the aforementioned story. Luis Santiago was a friend of mine as well as a fellow agent. What happened to him was a tragedy, and I certainly mean no disrespect to him or his memory. By contrast, I mean to honor him by telling the rest of his story.

On July 3, 1995, an inflammatory news article was published in a University of California San Diego campus newspaper called *Voz Fronteriza* (*Border Voice*). This piece of garbage published an article—written by someone calling himself "El Chingaso"—entitled "Death of a Migra Pig." The article cheered the death of Border Patrol Agent Luis Santiago and called for the killing of all Border Patrol agents (Chingaso, 1995).

Rep. Duncan Hunter was furious and demanded a retraction and apology from the university chancellor, Richard Atkinson. UC San Diego claimed it was not their place to apologize, and they were not responsible for what campus newspapers wrote. UCSD vice chancellor Joseph W. Watson said that any apology will have to come from the editors of the *Voz Fronteriza*. Editor Harry Barra also refused to apologize and tried to claim the article was actually a letter and certainly wasn't *his* fault.

Rep. Hunter stated he would start legislation to defund UCSD and any other institution that advocated the killing of American officers. I agreed and personally vowed never to allow a penny of my money to support that university in any way. I also read the piece in question and concluded that it was an article written by a reporter. It was not a letter, as claimed by the newspaper. It is nice to know how UCSD feels about America's first, and sometimes last, line of defense. What about all these hate speech laws we hear about? Are these the kinds of people that should be running a college university or editing a newspaper?

Think about that.

And So it Begins

The following events happened after the aforementioned article and were common knowledge at that time. The entire station talked about these occurrences frequently, including management, though they were never officially documented within the Patrol, as far as I know. Nor was the topic discussed lightly. Each newly reported event left the agents stunned, as each was simply unexplainable. The Brown Field Station at that time was possibly the largest station in the Border Patrol, and every agent knew of Agent (Trainee) Luis Santiago. No one thought that any of the following happenings were some kind of joke and, if they did, nobody was laughing.

I am not certain which agents were involved in the following incidents, but I am positive of the dates on which they happened. Once things started to happen, I recorded the dates each particular event occurred on. Some dates are from newspaper articles that also recorded some of the events.

This filthy *Voz Fronteriza* article, though, seemed to have stirred something in the spirit world up on Otay Mountain, including the cliff on top of Otay Lakes Dam. Oh sure, there had been the two incidents with my radio after Luis Santiago's death, but nothing like what happened next. These are the only encounters I personally know of, though I suspect there were plenty more.

First Encounter

Two or three days after the nasty article was published, I was assigned to our jail facility for processing. Bill, a friend of mine, was assigned with me to the "coralon." As usual, we were very busy, processing maybe four or five hundred prisoners during the shift. About midway through the night, Bill approached me, looking a bit pale, and said, "Hey Rocky, the prisoners over there just told me they saw Santiago up on the mountain."

I was puzzled by that. "What do you mean they saw Santiago up on the mountain?"

He repeated himself, "Tonight. They told me they saw Santiago up on the mountain!"

"Do you mean they're trying to say he's not really dead? Are they making jokes about his death?" I snapped.

"No. They saw his ghost on the trail leading from the White Cross, and they're still over there talking about it. They're pretty shaken up."

Apparently, Bill relayed, after an encounter with Santiago, the aliens stood frozen until agents tracked them down and took them into custody.

I was caught completely off guard by such a revelation and did not know what to say. Yet, I could tell by the look on Bill's face that he was not kidding. I went over to get a better look at the aliens claiming such a tale, and they did look plenty scared. At first, I thought maybe it was some agent with a sick sense of humor using the recent death to scare a few pollos; however, many times over and over this proved to absolutely not be the case.

This was just the beginning of one of the most bizarre episodes in the history of the U.S. Border Patrol. There were many more encounters to come. Soon, the aliens began to call him "el fantasma," the phantom agent. I have never heard of another series of incidents that ever came close to rivaling what was to follow.

Second Encounter

The White Cross ridgeline splits the US/Mexico border just east of where the international fence ends on Otay Mountain. On top of that ridgeline there used to be a white cross that stood about ten to twelve feet high, as best I remember. The cross actually stood a few feet on the American side of the border and was erected as a memorial for all the aliens who had died while trying to cross the mountain. At least, that is how things were set up in the 1990s.

Since that time, the cross has been taken down, whether because the fence has expanded farther up the mountain or for some other reason, I don't know. There is a saddle, meaning a low spot, that separates the White Cross ridgeline from the Otay Truck Trail. Most traffic during the 1990s originated from the White Cross and headed north on one of its many trails. There were no roads leading up to the cross at that time, and it took PAs about forty-five minutes to an hour to hike over to it. The area was more easily accessed from Mexico than from the U.S.

Most often, it was more effective to wait for the traffic to arrive at the Truck Trail, because an agent could not hike up to the White Cross without being detected by one of the many lookouts posted there by the smugglers. The lookout's job was to detect agents trying to cross the saddle on foot. In recent years, a road was built by the Bureau of Land Management that leads right up to where the cross once stood, so the groups of two and three hundred that once congregated there are now a thing of the past.

On July 15, 1995, four of us were working a group of aliens near the White Cross trail leading up to the Otay Truck Trail. It was a swing shift, and we were the only four agents assigned to the area: Mark, Miguel, Jack, and myself. We were waiting for a group of about thirty to come up to the road from the south, cross it, and drop down into Windmill Canyon.

Mark and I went maybe 300 feet down into Windmill Canyon to cut off their northern route. Miguel and Jack were on a high point overlooking the road. Once the group passed by, Miguel and Jack would fall in behind them, cutting off their southern escape route, and the group would be sandwiched between us. It was our favorite tactic, and very effective.

As the traffic started coming up to the road, Miguel called over the radio to Mark and me down below. "Hey, they're on the road now. Get ready," he said.

"Okay, we're in position," we replied.

A few moments went by and Miguel came back on the radio saying, "They just stopped on the road for some reason. They're just standing there."

"Okay, tell us when they start moving again."

We waited several minutes before asking, "Are they moving yet?"

"No, they're still just standing there. Something's going on," Miguel answered. "There's some kind of commotion. I think somebody stopped them." After a brief pause, he came back on the radio again. "We hear crying. You guys start back to the top, we're going over to them now and see what's up."

Mark and I left our positions and started hiking back up the canyon wall. It took several minutes to get back to Miguel and his partner's position. When we reached the illegals, the entire group was indeed just standing there in the road. Nobody tried to run off or make any other escape attempts. Some were still crying. The whole scene was strange. I had never seen a group just stand there and wait to be caught before.

Miguel and Jack, too, were unusually quiet and behaving like something was bothering them. Certainly, it was unusual for Miguel to be so quiet. Later, after the prisoners were loaded up and sent to the station for processing,

Miguel—an outgoing person not known for holding his tongue—said that when he and his partner approached the group they merely stood there in the road, crying. The illegals claimed they had been stopped exactly where Miguel found them by a phantom Border Patrol agent who identified himself as Luis Santiago. They said the deceased agent told them about his own death and the sadness he felt. Santiago then walked right up to the foot guide and informed him they could go no further. "Wait right here," he said and disappeared.

The guide did exactly that and didn't move until Miguel and Jack arrived and took them all into custody.

There were only four of us assigned to the mountain that night, and there was only one road accessing the mountain at that time. Miguel and Jack had an open view of the entire surrounding area. It is virtually impossible that some other Border Patrol agent snuck up on the mountain that night, hid in our area, and perpetrated some kind of hoax.

It just wasn't done.

Third Encounter

The very next night on July 16, 1995, Ricardo and his partner were working traffic on a trail north of the White Cross just below the Otay Truck Trail—the same trail we had worked the night before, only a little farther south. He and his partner Sam were unaware of the events the previous night, as Miguel, Jack, Mark, and I had told no one.

Ricardo said it was probably about 10:00 p.m. when he and Sam encountered thirty illegals just south of the road. Oddly enough, they were just standing on the trail right out in the open. The agents walked right up but nobody ran or tried to hide. They just stood there, frozen with fear, afraid to move.

"When we started talking to them," Ricardo relayed, "the aliens claimed that a phantom agent named Santiago walked up to them, carrying his head in his hands. Santiago's apparition proceeded to tell them about his own death. He said he was sad and could not yet pass on, implying that something was left unfinished."

"The Phantom Agent told us to stop here and wait," the aliens said.

Ricardo and Sam were both completely taken by surprise and grew angry. Ricardo yelled at the group, telling them to keep quiet. He accused them of lying and being disrespectful of the dead. "How could someone possibly talk without a head?" he demanded.

An alien replied, "He is a ghost; he can do whatever he wants."

The two agents insisted the group just shut up and say nothing else.

I only know of this incident because there was a vehicle shortage at the time, and I was partnered up to ride with Ricardo the very next night after this occurred. It was while we rode together that he told me about the incident.

It is of interest that Agent Santiago's death was indeed caused by a head injury during his fall off the cliff; however, it is extremely doubtful that graphic information like that would have been shared with newspapers. The fall was public knowledge. The specifics and gore of the landing were not.

It is also interesting to note that the groups always knew it was a spirit as he approached, yet none of them ever tried to run from the "Phantom Agent" until the last sighting. No living agent would be able to simply walk up to a group of illegals out in the open because if the aliens recognized that it was green traffic they would take off running every time. Sometimes a PA could walk up to a single person if he or she was lost or needed help, but a group would always quail. Always.

Fourth Encounter

On August 4, 1995, another unit from Patrol Group A once more encountered alien traffic stopped by a phantom agent up on the mountain, right at one of the White Cross trials leading to Truck Trail. These folks also referred to Santiago by name and said they knew he was a spirit. Like the others, they offered no resistance to the apprehending agents, nor did they try to run away.

It was strange.

187

Some of the guys on Patrol Group B and Patrol Group C were starting to have similar experiences. Since I was on Patrol Group A, it is mostly their stories of which I have personal knowledge, but I understand it was happening to all of us. The encounters involving the other patrol groups mostly came to me through the grapevine but, since I could not verify them, I have left those stories out. The possibility of some deranged living agent being responsible for these events was quickly dismissed, especially after the witnesses would describe the agent as "floating across the terrain."

"He does not walk as a normal agent," they would say.

Witnesses claimed that he was slightly transparent. I guess this is why they never ran. Apparently, they knew at first sight that he was no living person.

Of course, we considered the possibility that the guides were making these stories up and telling them to their human cargo, but some of the witnesses involved had no guides. Also, how would a smuggler profit from telling such a thing? Fear of encountering ghosts would have ruined a profitable journey and created fear to the point that people would no longer want to cross in the mountains. That meant losing business. Besides, every group that was caught landed at the immigration jail facility for processing with the smuggler facing possible jail time. So why would a smuggler bring a group of thirty aliens illegally into U.S., hike them up the mountain, and then frighten them into stopping and just standing there until the Border Patrol agents showed up to arrest them? He wouldn't! That is ridiculous. Moreover, his controller would have him killed; large groups meant big money.

Besides, it was usually the guides who were approached by the so-called phantom, and the guides were always caught when the phantom appeared. I think you will see, later, that it was virtually impossible that the smugglers were responsible for these incidents.

Fifth Encounter

On August 5, 1995, a different crew from Patrol Group A were working the mountain near the White Cross area. Manny and his two partners were attempting to intercept a group of illegals. The traffic managed to give them the slip and got by, so Manny and company were trying to catch up from behind.

The PAs pursued them up the trail and across the road and were about to drop down into Windmill Canyon when suddenly they ran into the traffic from behind. Inexplicably, all of the approximately thirty-five illegal aliens had simply stopped on the trail near the edge of the canyon wall—right out in the open, just like the others before them! It was almost the exact spot where our incident days before had taken place.

Manny later told me himself that, as he approached the foot guide at the front of the group, the man became hysterical. The guide dropped to his knees and fell down to the ground crying, repeating Santiago's name several times over and over.

Once again, several nights in a row on the same trail, aliens were stopped and denied passage by a phantom Border Patrol agent. I have no idea how often this was happening to the other units on our patrol group or to the guys on Patrol Group B and Patrol Group C; I only know that it was.

One thing was for sure, though: The entire station knew of the phantom and was talking openly about him, including management. Nobody was laughing or cracking jokes about it, either. Everyone took it quite seriously, but none of us knew what to make of it.

After August 5th, the smugglers and guides stopped using the White Cross as a staging area almost entirely—at least after dark anyways. We even heard feedback from some of the guides themselves confirming that they were too afraid to cross that area of the mountain and started using different routes. They did not want to risk encountering El Fantasma again. Some of the agents, too, were starting to avoid working that area of the mountain.

A few years later, somebody let it slip that Luis Santiago had actually been pushed off the cliff at Otay Lakes Dam on that fateful night and even knew who may have done it. This was no real surprise to anyone. It was exactly what most of us had believed all along.

Here is something to think about. A guide or smuggler taking his group of illegals across to Otay Lakes Dam would likely start from the area that was currently being haunted. Guides only work the specific trails and routes they are allowed to work and have one or two canyons they share with a handful of other foot guides. If they start intruding on another smuggler's route without permission from their bosses, it often cost them their lives. We found bodies of dead foot-guides who got crossways with other smugglers all the time.

If Agent Santiago was indeed murdered at Otay Lakes Dam like I believe he was, then the smuggler who did it was likely leading groups starting from the White Cross area—the same area where they were being stopped by a so called ghost agent.

As bizarre as it sounds, is seems possible that the foot guide who fell to his knees screaming Santiago's name was actually the one who shoved him of the cliff. If that is actually what happened.

Still, the whole series of events is so unbelievable and so hard to fathom that anything is possible, if any of this is to be believed at all.

Sixth Encounter

Sometime in late August during the hot summer months, the sightings shifted to a new area. A couple of agents apprehended a group of aliens coming down from a peak called the 562 hill. This peak went from sea level and rose to almost 1800 feet, so it was no easy chore getting up it. Several unfortunate souls had died from heat stroke trying to cross that hill in the summer time.

The 562 hill stood between the Otay Mountain and Otay Valley/Dam Canyon. Groups heading towards the lake dam would often take this route to get there.

The group of aliens involved in this particular encounter told the arresting agents how they had gotten separated from their guide the night before. They were hopelessly lost and out of water and could have easily died as many others had before. The party then claimed that they were approached by Border Patrol Agent Santiago.

"An agent stopped us last night," they said, "but he didn't seem real. We could see through him. The phantom pointed to a trail and told us to follow it."

"'You will find water on the other side,' he told us. Then he disappeared into the night,'" they all said.

The group did as instructed and, just as the phantom claimed, found water.

Unlike other witnesses who were terrified by the encounters, this bunch was thankful. When the agents tracked them down, the aliens were quite glad to see them. "The phantom saved our lives," they said.

It is interesting to note that this group was without a smuggler.

Seventh Encounter

On October 14, 1995, one of my academy classmates Alan was sitting in his vehicle on the 680 road a little north of the border fence. The 680 road sits on Otay Mesa at the base of Otay Mountain. A night scope was set up on a hill a mile or so away, directly behind his position, and the scope operator had a clear view of the entire area. It was a cool, pleasant evening, and the agent was sitting in his Bronco with the windows rolled down.

Sometime around midnight, Alan was startled by a loud scream just outside his driver's side door. Immediately, he jumped out and started shining his flashlight around, but saw nothing. The startled PA radioed the scope operator and asked him to look around. "Especially near my vehicle," he said.

The scope operator took a look, but couldn't see anything either. "All is quiet," he reported. "There is no traffic anywhere on the mesa."

But, when Alan keyed his vehicle radio mic again, the radio went crazy. These radios have an LED readout that tells what channel it is on. It spells out the frequency, such as BRF8, BRF9, etc. However, the radio just began to scroll words and letters in an unintelligible manner for about a minute. Just gibberish. When it stopped, it spelled out "Santiago." The radio then promptly went dead and would not reboot.

By coincidence, there was a frequency zone that bore the agent's name in San Diego sector, but it wasn't a frequency we used and it took a couple of tricky manual adjustments to change the radio to that zone. The vehicle was turned over to the garage in order to repair the radio, but the mechanics were unable to fix it. It had to be completely replaced.

This particular classmate, oddly enough, was the last person to talk to Agent Santiago on the radio before he died. Alan knew of my own experience with my radio the night of Santiago's passing and the night of his funeral and said he was comfortable telling me this because he didn't think I would ridicule him.

Eighth Encounter

Between November 1995 and January 1996, aliens began reporting that a phantom Border Patrol agent was stopping them on top of the cliffs near Otay Lakes Dam. No longer were the reported sightings on Otay Mountain; now they were confined only to the cliffs next to the dam at Otay Lakes.

The ghost had moved.

One evening shortly before dusk, I went to the dam to observe the area for possible traffic. As I approached the dam, I ran head-on into about ten or fifteen illegals with their smuggler. No sensors had been activated, so I had no idea anyone was even in the area. I would never purposely work a group so close to the cliffs, especially now, and I was within fifty feet of the cliff when I bumped into them.

It was a chance encounter. The guide was out in front, and we both froze for a second just looking at each other, each of us clearly taken a bit by surprise. The guide was a slightly older man, forty or so, and his hair was just starting to gray. Older smugglers were often the most dangerous and usually had the longest and most violent criminal records.

I gave him a command to get down on the ground, but he refused. I had expected that, however. I could tell by the look on his face he was going to try me. A smuggler typically would not stare an agent in the eye unless he was going do something crazy. This scumbag knew that I was alone, while he had plenty of followers with him. Without question, the followers will do whatever the smuggler tells them to do, even if he tells them to jump the agent.

Suddenly, the smuggler ran directly towards the top of the cliff, but then slowed down, looking back to see if I was chasing him as if trying to lure me between the group and the cliff. What a piece of human filth, I thought.

I immediately wondered, was this how Luis Santiago was lured to the cliff? Instantly, I was angry, but managed to keep my wits. There was no way I was getting any closer to that cliff—not with so many suspects around me.

At that time, we were still carrying revolvers. I drew it, but I did not have enough rounds chambered to shoot all of them without reloading if they decided to charge me and shove me towards the edge.

I eventually got the upper hand. I was not able to get the smuggler, but I was able to take his human cargo and deny him a paycheck. I made them all get down on the ground and approach my position on their hands and knees, threatening to shoot anyone who dared to stand up because, by that time, I was within twenty feet of the cliff. After the guide's antics, I was in no mood to take any chances.

The smuggler, of course, took off and ran across the cliff top. As I watched him run, I could not help but hope he would slip and fall over the edge. Oh, I know what you are thinking: What a horrible thought to have about somebody.

Well, that is because the average person does not know foot guides and smugglers like I do. All of them have murdered people they were leading and have raped the women in their care. Even the very young girls traveling with them are not spared. I'm the one who found the bodies and tried to comfort terrified women. So, I don't really care if that thought fails on the Politically Correct Richter. They are junkies and their brains have been cooked, fried beyond repair from years of drug abuse and crime. These monsters have truly become sub-human zombies in every sense of the word. If you could look into their eyes, you would know what I am talking about, and I can tell you with all certainty that this smuggler scumbag would have done me in if given the opportunity.

This leads me back to a point we discussed earlier about how illegals are taken down. An agent doesn't just catch a group of aliens, and they certainly don't just give up. They are always led by someone, as they themselves are just followers and will obey whoever is leading them, like sheep, which is why the smugglers call them "pollos." The smugglers and guides have total control, and the followers will do whatever they are told. So, it is not about catching individuals, it is about taking down the leader and taking his group from him by force. This is a transition of power.

Many times, the guide will abandon his group and try to run away; other times he goes down with them. Even if he stays, he will usually try to show that he is still in charge, which is very dangerous for the agent, especially if an agent is alone. The guide may quietly tell the group things like, "Watch, I'll make the agent give us water. I'll make him give us food."

The agent must not fall for this. Giving water to thirsty aliens is fine, but never because the guide tells you to. The agent must control the guide, if he knows who it is. If he controls the guide, he controls the group. If he does not, he may find himself getting jumped by the entire bunch and maybe even disarmed. Therefore, any agent standing too close to a cliff would be in great peril if the smuggler orders the "pollos" to shove him over.

After this incident, all doubt left me that Santiago's death was an accident.

Field Operations Supervisor Encounter

A month or so went by and we changed from swing shift to midnight shift. I actually liked working graveyard shift better than evenings, but this particular night I was assigned "Desk Officer Duties."

I was not happy. I should have banged in sick! I thought, fuming.

Desk officer was the worst assignment there was. An agent was stuck all night in a cubicle answering the phone, counting inventory, monitoring the radio, and doing meaningless reports. Usually, the agent was in the office by himself or herself with no one to talk to. It was very boring. If the desk officer was lucky, a supervisor might come for a few minutes to talk or make sure the unfortunate soul was still awake. Even if a supervisor just came in to give a butt-chewing about something, it was a welcome relief just to break the monotony.

Earlier that night during muster, the Field Operations Supervisor for the shift had warned the PAs about dozing off while on duty. Everyone who works midnights eventually dozes off from time to time. We just say, "The Z Monster gotcha." And, believe me, it got all of us. If someone ever claims otherwise, he or she is lying, plain and simple.

Nevertheless, the FOS reminded everyone to stay awake or be written up for disciplinary action. Sometime around three or four in the morning, the FOS came in to check on me.

Fortunately I was still awake.

Ironically, the FOS said, "I'm having trouble staying awake tonight, so I thought I better get up and move around a bit. Otherwise, I'll have to write myself up for sleeping, and that would be embarrassing."

The FOS hung around and we talked for a while. It was actually a pretty slow night up to that point and not much was going on. While we were talking, however, a group was detected near Otay Lakes Dam and called out on the radio.

After hearing the radio call, the FOS said, "I hope they don't work that."

"Why's that?" I asked.

"May God rest his soul, but I know for a fact that Luis Santiago is still patrolling up on that cliff at the dam," he replied. "I just prefer that everyone stay away from there."

"So, you believe the stories?" I asked.

"Oh, I have no doubt whatsoever about the stories," he said.

The FOS stopped short of saying he had seen the apparition himself, but seemed to be alluding to it.

Actually, several aliens had fallen from that same cliff in the past. Agent Santiago was not the first to fall from there. So, I knew he really just wanted

195

the agents to back off the area and work the traffic away from the lake, though sometimes that was hard to do successfully. Some supervisors even became somewhat paranoid about that area and if a PA was trying to work traffic anywhere near there, he or she would get on the radio and call them off the group. They would tell them, "Work it somewhere else."

It happened to me once, even though I was quite a safe distance from the dam. I fully realized that working aliens close to the dam was too risky for everyone involved, but I was not willing to concede the entire area to the smugglers just because some things out of the ordinary were happening.

Ninth Encounter

On January 21, 1996, Agent Echelmeyer and her partner were assigned to the Otay Lakes area. She was working the midnight shift and I believe she was on Patrol Group C at that time. Around five o'clock in the morning, though still under hours of darkness, she was alerted to a pair of suspected illegal aliens on top of the dam. Echelmeyer and her partner were already sitting blacked out in the park a couple of hundred yards away, so they responded. No other Border Patrol agents were in the area.

There are three or four different trails the pair could have followed from the dam. The agents chose one and hoped the aliens would come their way. A moment or two later, two illegals appeared, walking directly for the concealed agents. The pair was talking out loud, not at all caring if they were detected. Without hesitation, the two walked right up to Echelmeyer and her partner and turned themselves in!

One said, "We knew you were waiting for us."

Agent Echelmeyer asked, "How did you know we were waiting right here?'

An alien answered, "The phantom agent on top of the cliff by the dam told us you were here waiting for us, and that we should come over and give ourselves up."

Patrol Group A was the day shift relief for that six-week period, and my assignment for that day was also Otay Lakes. I ran into some of the off-going midnight agents that morning, and they told me of the occurrence within hours of it happening. Actually, the entire station was aware of the situation by day's end.

Efforts were made to determine if there was indeed another BP unit by the dam because things were now moving from the bizarre to the downright dangerous. If an agent was up there messing around on top of the cliff, there would be consequences. However, it was determined that no other PAs were anywhere near the area. If another agent had been by the dam, he would have taken the aliens into custody himself. He would never send them a couple hundred yards away and just tell them to turn themselves into somebody else.

Now, I want to say a few things about agent Gayle Echelmeyer. She was three classes ahead of me, was well respected, and very well liked. She was one of the most credible agents at Brown Field. If she said, "It was so," it was so! Gayle had the kind of reputation where her word was not questioned. She was an intelligent, no nonsense woman who promoted quickly through the ranks. Although many of the agents promoted into management are just that—managers, and not much else—Gayle had good leadership skills, and agents respected her opinion. She never forgot what is was like to be a field agent and always looked out for them. That is one of the reasons she was so well thought of. Most importantly, she was a good human being and a natural leader, so no one doubted her account of the incident.

In fact, Agent Echelmeyer's experience became the most well-known encounter of all the ghost sightings. Eventually she was promoted to the Patrol Agent In Charge of the Jacksonville, Florida Border Patrol Station. Sadly, in 2009 she passed away after a battle with cancer. She is still missed by all who knew her.

After that sighting, I decided to hang around the park for a while. This really got me thinking about what had happened to Luis and what these sightings were all about. I looked the canyon over with the binoculars for a while, thinking a group might be staging in the bottom waiting for dark. I even walked down the trail near the dam to check out a cave where aliens sometimes hid. As I walked the canyon bottom towards the cave, I passed by the very large rock where agent Santiago had landed after falling that night. Many of the items the emergency crews had used on him were still there on the ground— sheets, bandages, rubber gloves. Seeing those things still there was like a fresh kick in the gut. I felt very melancholy after that walkabout, so I climbed back to the top of the dam and left the entire area.

The Final Encounter

January 21, 1996, later in the evening of that same day, an alert was sent out that a group of fifteen was heading for the Otay Lakes dam. (One newspaper that covered this event reports the incident as happening on January 22, just after midnight. Personally, I believe an hour or so before midnight on January 21, 1996, is the correct time and date.) Arlo, a classmate of Luis Santiago and myself, responded to the area.

There are two versions to the story.

According to the newspaper, Arlo allowed the group to pass him by and began to tail them. At some point, he commanded them to stop and sit down. Instead of following the agent's orders, nine of them ran away. Arlo chased them, firing his gun, and caused six illegals to go over the edge of the cliff, killing one at the scene. Five survived the fall.

This is what the newspaper reported. So, this became the "official" story.

Interestingly enough, that paper did not say the person killed was an "undocumented immigrant" as it usually did. This time, the headline read, "Border Fugitive Plunges to Death" (Finz, 1996).

Maybe that means something, maybe it doesn't, but I can tell you for sure that when a group takes flight, the foot guide is the first to run. The rest of the group will play follow the leader and run right behind him. It is almost a certainty that the smuggler went over the cliff first and was the one killed.

The following five landed on top of him, which broke their fall somewhat. The five were severely injured, and I heard one of them died later, but I am not positive about that.

However, I learned the real story from the agents who were actually working that night. They said that when Arlo arrived at the scene, there was already chaos. He told the investigators six people had already gone over the cliff and nine were still on top screaming for help. Arlo called for more agents to come to the scene and help him with the rescue effort.

When everyone reported back to the station, Arlo came under scrutiny. His firearm was taken from him and the FBI was called in to investigate Arlo's actions. They took his weapon and tested it and his hands for gunpowder residue. Naturally, this was reported in the newspaper, who quickly tried to pin the whole thing on Arlo.

Not far from the Otay Lakes Dam is a water treatment facility. Some of their employees were outside working at the time this event occurred. They all reported hearing no gunshots whatsoever, though they were within easy hearing distance if there had been shots.

Not surprisingly, the investigation went nowhere. The FBI's efforts to pin it on Arlo actually backfired. The gunpowder residue test cleared Arlo, and so did the lineup!

What I have just told you is a combination of facts, testing, alien testimony, and agent testimony—all normal events in an investigation. But, what I am about to tell you now is an account personally told to me by an agent much senior to myself shortly before he retired.

I was off duty at the time this event occurred and was not involved in any part of the investigation; therefore, I am in no way claiming that what I am about to tell you is factual. However, I had received information in the past from this agent, and it had always proven accurate. If that is the case, then perhaps there is documentation of these events somewhere. I don't know. It could be logged somewhere in the FBI's X-files for all I know, but without a doubt the investigation was dead in the water.

Senior Agent's Version

Where this investigation supposedly takes an unexpected turn is when everyone returned to the station. The story goes like this:

The FBI was all set to hook up Arlo. He was guilty and he was their guy, but they tested his hands and his gun and both results were negative. He had not fired a weapon that night.

All nine uninjured aliens were interviewed and processed at the station. After that, they were sent to view a lineup with Arlo in it. None of the aliens identified him as the culprit. So, the FBI proceeded to line up everybody that was working that night. Still, no one was chosen as the guilty party. However, the surviving aliens insisted they could identify the guilty agent if they could just see him. Pictures of agents who were not on duty that night were brought in and shown. Still there were no takers.

Finally, one of the PAs assisting with the investigation went out into memorial hallway where the pictures of all the fallen agents from the Brown Field Station are hanging on the wall. He took down Luis Santiago's picture and brought it to the FBI, who then presented it to the survivors.

When the investigating FBI agents asked the witnesses if this was the Border Patrol agent who had chased them and fired his gun, every single one said yes! "He was shooting at us and chased us towards the cliff!" they cried.

The FBI agents, now thinking the case was solved, said, "Let's go get him."

The PA who had brought the picture shook his head. "We can't."

"Why not?" asked the investigators.

"Because that is Agent Luis Santiago," he explained. "Santiago was killed on that cliff last year."

If this last revelation I have just shared holds any truth, it starts to clear up a lot of things. Many other sightings and events begin to make sense. First of all, the sightings abruptly stopped. I continued to serve at the Brown Field Station for almost twelve more years, and I never again heard of another sighting of Santiago or the Phantom Agent—not by agents, not by aliens. The entire episode of events and sightings lasted approximately seven months. The sightings had started near the White Cross area and proceeded in a linear fashion to what we called the 562 hill, then finally made it to the Otay Lakes Dam where they ended, which is one of the exact routes groups used to reach the Otay dam. It is not the only route, but it is a common one.

At some point during the time these events were happening, or shortly thereafter, some of the agents contacted the *Coast to Coast AM* late night radio show hosted by Art Bell. It was a popular show among the guys, and I used to listen to it every night when I was assigned the midnight shift.

One night, *Coast to Coast* did a segment on the Phantom Border Patrol Agent that was haunting Otay Mountain and Otay Lakes Dam. I did not hear the show myself, so I do not know if Mr. Bell actually interviewed Border Patrol agents on the air or merely spoke about the information given to him beforehand. I wish I could have heard the broadcast. I am certain there are many other sightings that I have not heard about, some of which are still only known to the PAs personally involved.

An Eye For An Eye

After serving thirteen years at the Brown Field Station, I transferred to the Kingsville Station at Kingsville, Texas. Everyone there had to ride double. Nobody was allowed to ride alone when working anywhere outside the checkpoint.

One night while working the midnight shift, I was paired up with a new agent named Joe. He only had a couple of months in the field, but he seemed like a pretty good guy, so I didn't mind riding with him. Normally, having to ride with a partner bugged me. I much preferred riding solo because I was used to it.

During the ride, Joe and I started to talk. He was full of questions. He asked how long I had been in, where I was from, that kind of thing. Then he asked, "Have you served at any other stations?"

"Yeah, I was at Brown Field, San Diego Sector, for thirteen years," I said.

Right away, he was interested. "I have classmates there!" he said. "My classmates told me of an agent who was killed by falling off a cliff, but his ghost was still seen there. Did you ever hear about that?"

"Yes I did. He was my classmate," I said, "but the apparition is not seen anymore."

"Why?"

"I don't know," I admitted, but then relayed all the past events to him. We had a long night ahead of us, and he was very interested in hearing all the same things I have told you, the reader, thus far. I told him it was ruled an accident, but later I heard he was pushed to his death by a smuggler, which is what I had believed all along. I told him how it all started with the nasty article called "Death of a Migra Pig," then the many different sightings, and the final sightings at the Otay Lake dam. Then, I told him the senior agent's version of how a group supposedly claimed he chased them off the same cliff he fell from, killing one of them. I told him that was the last time anyone ever reported seeing him.

The young agent said, "Do you know what I think?"

"Not yet," I answered.

"Well, I think the reason the sightings stopped that night is because what you said was probably true. Also, what that senior agent told you is probably true. Your classmate was murdered, and since nothing was done about it, his ghost stayed and looked for the killer. When Santiago chased that group off the cliff that last night, the first one that went over was probably the guy who had killed him. He got revenge on the smuggler who shoved him the night he died, and now he can rest. That's why he's never been seen again."

I hadn't thought about that.

Well, I had to admit, Joe's theory made more sense than anything else I had heard throughout the entire chain of events. It is an insight I had not thought of before. It is true that the same guides used that pathway by the dam over and over again, so it would be a fitting end to what had possibly been the strangest series of events in Border Patrol history.

My Personal Belief

Now it is my turn. I would like to give my personal opinion and beliefs on what was really going on concerning the many reported sightings of the "Phantom Agent" or Luis Santiago's ghost. I believe there are two types of so-called hauntings: residual and intelligent.

A residual haunting, as I mentioned before, is where a scene is replayed over and over, whether anyone is there to see it or not. For example, a very tragic or emotional event happens, resulting in someone's untimely death, and the energy is imprinted and stored in the surrounding environment. When that happens, certain atmospheric conditions come about, such as weather, fog, humidity, static electricity, with a background of darkness, and the earth itself replays the tragic event, producing an apparition.

Even Christ himself said: "And he answered and said unto them, I tell you that if these should hold their peace, the stones would immediately cry out." (Luke 19 verse 40, King James Bible.)

When Cain killed his brother Abel, the earth itself recorded the murder and cried out for justice. (Genesis 4:10) "The voice of your brother's blood is crying to Me from the ground."

An intelligent haunting is when the apparition interacts with the person witnessing the event. All known sightings of Agent Santiago were interactive and intelligent. Actually, nearly every sighting of apparitions or spirits in the whole of the Otay area were interactive and intelligent hauntings.

Now, I must confess, since I am a Christian, I do not actually believe that a person's spirit is just left to wander the earth after death. The Bible tells us after death you will continue on to your final destination where you will be judged by God. It does not say that you will continue roaming the earth, visiting and talking with people. However, the Bible also tells us plainly that there are spirits who are cursed to aimlessly roam the earth until the final judgment day, and these spirits like being around people or inside of them if they can manage that. They especially like messing with people and scaring them.

I have heard so-called "experts" on this subject claim that limestone, granite, and water increases these poltergeist-type activities. Indeed, there is a lot of granite on Otay Mountain. Actually, I think the whole mountain is made of granite. Oftentimes, there is a heavy fog on the mountain after dark, as well. Of the two incidents I experienced, water or heavy fog was involved in both.

I have heard theologians say that all ghost activity is actually an inhumane spirit mimicking a real person who has passed away. I don't know if the sightings of Santiago's ghost was or wasn't the spirit of my friend, classmate, and fellow agent. I believe perhaps it was a disembodied spirit impersonating Luis Santiago. I firmly believe many such spirits inhabit the entire Otay area and they are restless for some unexplainable reason.

I swear, sometimes, I could just feel the presence of evil on the mountain, Otay Valley, and Marron Valley. Once, the mountain burned in a wildfire. After the fire, I did not notice that feeling of evil nearly so much. It was almost as if the flames had cleansed the mountain of the spiritual presence.

Still, something definitely was not right with that mountain.

Chapter 16

The Curse
of Brown Field

Lives Cut Short

From the time I began to serve at the Brown Field Station to the time of this writing, there have been ten deaths there, five of them by suicide.

On July 5th, 1998, Danny Medina was working a swing shift as a new trainee at the Brown Field Station. Around six or seven in the evening, he walked into the locker room and found an agent lying motionless on the floor towards the back of the room. He was unsure if the man was actually injured, dead, or just messing with him.

It was actually quite common for more experienced guys to torment and mess with the trainees. If a newbie was the kind of person who wore his feelings on his shirtsleeve, then the Border Patrol was not for him.

Danny hurried back out into the hallway and asked another trainee for help. Both of them went back in the locker room to where the agent was lying on the floor and discovered immediately it was no prank. Soon, the locker room was filled with people trying to find out what happened.

A single gunshot wound was discovered directly over the heart of the deceased. It was self-inflicted. Supervisory Border Patrol Agent Jim Bendorf had committed suicide, shooting himself once in the heart.

I will not go into why he may have done this, but he had suffered numerous on-duty injuries during his many years of service in the Border Patrol. Jim Bendorf had an illustrious and near legendary career. He spent many nights out on foot patrolling and hunting bandits. Once during a fierce firefight, he was shot and seriously wounded. He had been injured many other times as well.

Actually, injuries were the norm at Brown Field. Year after year, Brown Field ranked number one in agent injuries and deaths. It is the only station to ever have more injuries than the academy. I was injured there numerous times myself and will probably have knee and back trouble for the rest of my life as a result.

Agent Bendorf's locker was very near my own, and I had to walk right by it every day to get to my things. When Agent Bendorf shot himself, he had leaned back against his locker. The bullet did not completely penetrate through his body, but had made an indentation into the door of his locker. For whatever reason, the station did not fix or replace the locker door.

Every day for the remainder of the time that I was at Brown Field, I would walk by and see the bullet indention in his locker. It served as a grim but important reminder not to take this job, or anything else in life, too seriously.

This line of work eats its own. It can suck the life right out of you, magnifying small problems until they seem too large to overcome. One must learn to see everything as funny; even a gallows sense of humor can serve you well. Yet, I see so many agents who are just way too serious. I always tell them nothing is serious but your safety. Any day you go home is a good day.

Trainee Medina, the agent who found Bendorf, went on to become a top agent and was well known for his ability to hike up and down the mountain all day long. The "Mountain Goat," we called him. After several years of service, he was promoted to a supervisor position.

On August 31, 2013, Supervisory Border Patrol Agent Danny Medina committed suicide with his service firearm at home. He was the fifth Border Patrol agent that worked or had served at the Brown Field Station, to commit suicide. It was quite ironic that Danny Medina who, as a trainee, had been the agent to discover the body of the first agent to commit suicide at the Brown Field Station, then became the latest victim himself, while serving in the very same supervisory capacity.

Actually, at the time of this writing, suicide seems to be the Border Patrol's number one problem. Suicide for the general public is about twelve per 100,000. For law enforcement, it averages twenty per 100,000. However, for the Border Patrol it runs well over thirty per 100,000. At least, those are the statistics that I have read. For the Border Patrol, I believe the actual numbers may be much higher than the statistics mentioned above.

The largest the Patrol has ever been is about 20,000 agents, although I doubt we have ever actually reached that number. Yet, I personally know of at least ten agents off the top of my head who have committed suicide. That would make fifty or sixty per 100,000 more realistic.

Jim Bendorf and Danny Medina both committed suicide while working at the Brown Field Station, as did a third agent that I did not personally know. Jeff Ryan and James Perkins both committed suicide after leaving the Brown Field Station.

This is a complex issue at best, and each man's circumstances were different. I will make no further comment on this matter, as some of these men were my friends.

Saying Goodbye to Jesse and Tommy

At 11:00 p.m. on October 20, 1998, Field Operations Supervisor McDermott solemnly stepped up to the podium to address the troops for the midnight muster briefing. We immediately knew something was wrong. Mr. McDermott was a very gruff talking man with a heavy New York accent. Supervisors feared him, but field agents loved him. He could chew an agent out like no other, but we liked him and respected him. He deeply cared about his people, and we all knew it. Yet, despite the many butt-chewings he gave, I had never seen this look on his face before.

On this night, Mr. McDermott stepped to the podium and said, "I have some very bad news to relay about two of your fellow agents. Tonight, Tommy Williams and Jesse De La Osa were both killed in a vehicle accident. It is a horrible day."

The FOS then left the podium, turning it over to a supervisor for the remainder of the briefing, but there was nothing left to be said. Jesse and Tommy were friends, and it was indeed a horrible day.

Tommy and Jesse had been on a temporary assignment to Artesia, New Mexico. They were killed on the last day of their detail when they were hit head-on by another driver that had lost control of her car on a slippery road. The woman driving the other car was also killed.

That night, another agent and I were sent to Jesse's house to pull guard duty, while his widowed wife tried to sleep. Jesse and his wife were in the process of moving into their brand new home, but Jesse had yet to spend a single night in it. I could not even imagine the pain his family was feeling.

The next night, I was sent to pull guard duty at the hotel where some of Tommy's family was staying. His family had flown in from out of state after receiving the bad news about their loved one. It was an honor to be sent to watch over Jesse and Tommy's families in their most difficult hour, but it is an honor that I wish had never been necessary.

In four months, we had lost three agents. Nineteen ninety-eight was a very bad year for the Brown Field Station. A short time after I left San Diego Sector for Texas, I received notice that another Brown Field agent had been killed on duty.

On March 30, 2008, Border Patrol Agent Jarod Dittman was killed in some type of vehicle collision while patrolling in his assigned area. The driver who hit him was completely at fault and fled the scene. The culprit was never caught. Agent Dittman was a newer agent. I did not know him well, but we had served briefly on the same patrol group.

Knowing how many agents were killed on duty while serving at Brown Field and the number of suicides there, has led people to wonder if there was a curse on that station. Like I said, to my knowledge, no station has had so many agents killed on duty, or die while serving, than the Brown Field Border Patrol Station. This does not include several more Brown Field agents who died off duty from causes such as cancer.

So is it cursed? I don't know.

I enjoyed my time at Brown Field and always thought myself fortunate to be there. In its day, it was considered the best station in the entire Border Patrol. I just thought it was a very dynamic place to be and respected the very dangerous terrain. Yet, since others have begun to voice their opinions concerning the possibility of a curse, I researched and compared Brown Field injuries and deaths to other stations. The results are unsettling, to say the least.

It does make me wonder.

Chapter 17
End of Watch
And So the Sun Sets

During my career, I was temporarily detailed to as many as ten different stations and permanently assigned to three stations in three different states and sectors: San Diego, California; Kingsville, Texas; and Tucson, Arizona, in that order—but I did not experience or hear of many paranormal experiences in any of these other stations. I did hear of one story in Kingsville, Texas, in which several agents had seen a male apparition ride a bicycle down a dirt road. That is actually kind of funny, if you think about it! There were a few third and fourth hand stories, as I mentioned before, but I have elected to leave most of those stories out because verification of those incidents was not possible.

Every other event took place in Marron Valley, Otay Mountain, and Otay Valley, San Diego Sector, California. It just seemed like there was some bad mojo in that area. I never felt that way about any other place I ever worked. Oh sure, plenty of bad things happened in all the other stations' areas of operation as well, but the Otay and Tecate Mountains were unique. Working in these areas are what made this book possible.

Now, before any of you would-be-ghost-hunters go running up to Otay Mountain for a paranormal experience, please keep one thing in mind: This is still a very active area for illegal alien crossings and criminal activities. These paranormal experiences and ghost stories are a collection of events that involved over 500 agents and occurred over a thirteen-year period. The chances of anybody going up on the mountain or into Marron Valley on any given night and having a paranormal experience is virtually zero. However, the chance of somebody going up there at night and encountering a very real illegal alien or bandit or some other criminal and becoming one of a very long list of victims is quite high. This is no place to mess around, especially after dark.

Many of these stories took place before the mountain burned off in a wildfire in 1996. As I said earlier, it seems as if the fire cleansed the mountain of much of the evil presence. Most of the happenings in this book took place very early in my career, and before that fire.

We have all heard it said, "There is nothing in the dark that is not there in the light."

Yet, I would like to leave you with a different thought to ponder because, I can assure you, sometimes there are things in the dark that are not there in the light!

10-42: The End of Watch

More Border Patrol agents have been killed in the line of duty than all other federal agencies combined. From 1924 to 1994 when I entered on duty, forty-seven Border Patrol agents had been killed on duty. In the twenty years I served, seventy-four more perished. In total, 122 agents have been killed on duty as of this writing.

This is the End of Watch for those of the San Diego Sector who I knew either personally or by story.

This book is dedicated to all agents everywhere who have lost their lives in service both on duty or while performing off duty as well. For many of them perished while intervening during a crime, assisting other law enforcement, responding to natural disasters, and while trying to protect innocent lives. Each hero has a story to tell.

Fallen Agents

Brown Field Station:
Luis A. Santiago—March 28, 1995
James Bendorf –July 5, 1998
Jesus De La Ossa—October 20, 1998
Thomas J. Williams–October 20, 1998
Jarod Dittman—March 30, 2008

Imperial Beach Station:
Catherine M. Hill—October 25, 2002

There was an Imperial Beach Border Patrol agent that chased several suspects into the river, on the border, and contracted Hepatitis C from the water as a result. He died off duty at a later time as a result of his on duty exposure. I am sad to say that although I knew of his story, I never knew his name.

Chula Vista Station:
Roberto J. Duran—May 6, 2002

El Cajon Station:
Stephen C. Starch—June 14, 1997
Stephen M. Sullivan—March 27, 1999

Boulevard (Campo) Station:
Eric Cabral—July 26, 2007

I urge you to visit the www.borderpatrolmuseum.com agent memorials page and read about them all. Better yet, go to the Border Patrol Museum in El Paso, Texas, and read about each one in the Memorial Library. They deserve it.

Conclusion

Our way of life, and civilization itself, is possible only because of the thin blue or green line that runs through and around our nation and the rest of the civilized world. If this line ever completely broke down for more than just a few hours or days at most, you and your family would be robbed, murdered, and viciously victimized without mercy. Such crimes would occur on a regular basis. Even though the police often arrive too late to stop most crimes in progress, just the fact that a police force exists is enough to keep chaos in check.

So be aware that while you slumber the night away, there are men and women you have never met walking trails and canyons in total darkness, often alone, in places you have never heard of, for the sole purpose of protecting our peace. This they do all night long, every single night, with little or no fanfare. So, if tonight, you are able to take your rest peacefully in your bed, take a moment to remember the sacrifices of the men and women on the list above who are taking their rest in eternity.

END

Works Cited

(CNN), L. A. (1997, February 28). *Botched L.A. Bank Heist Turns Into Bloody Shootout*. (C. Interactive, Producer) Retrieved from U.S. News Story Page: http://archive.org/web/20070522160925/http://www.cnn.com/US/9702/28/shootout.update/index.html

Avalanche-Journal. (1997, June 15). *Lubbock Family Mourns Death of Border Patrol Agent*. Retrieved from Avalanche-Journal: http://lubbockonline.com/news/061697/lubbock.htm

Chingaso, E. (1995, May). Death of a Migra Pig. *Voz Fronteriza (Border Voice), Vol. XX No. 2.*

Finz, S. (1996, March 21). Border Fugitive Plunges to Death. *San Diego Union Tribune, Congressional Record Volume 142, Number 40.*

Protection, U. C. (1999, 03 27). *Stephen M. Sullivan*. Retrieved from Official Website of the Department of Homeland Security: http://www.cbp.gov/about/in-memoriam/stephen-m-sullivan

Printed in Great Britain
by Amazon